William Moffat
A History of Scotland
Book Four

Oxford University Press 1985

Oxford University Press, Walton Street, Oxford OX2 6DP

Oxford   London
New York   Toronto   Melbourne   Auckland
Kuala Lumpur   Singapore   Hong Kong   Tokyo
Delhi   Bombay   Calcutta   Madras   Karachi
Nairobi   Dar es Salaam   Cape Town

and associated companies in
Beirut   Berlin   Ibadan   Mexico City   Nicosia

Oxford is a trade mark of Oxford University Press

British Library Cataloguing in Publication Data
Moffat, William
A History of Scotland.
Bk. 4
1. Scotland – History
I. Title
941.1   DA762
ISBN 0-19-917056-8

A History of Scotland

		Hardback	Paperback
Book 1	*Earliest times to the last of the Celtic kings*	0 19 917053 3	0 19 917042 8
Book 2	*The Normans to the House of the High Steward*	0 19 917054 1	0 19 917043 6
Book 3	*James I to Restoration*	0 19 917055 X	0 19 917044 4
Book 4	*The Restoration to the Victorians*	0 19 917056 8	0 19 917051 7
Book 5	*Modern Times*	0 19 917064 9	0 19 917063 0

Phototypeset by Tradespools Ltd., Frome, Somerset
Printed in Hong Kong

Contents

The Return of the King

By 1652 Scotland had no government or army of its own, even its new Church was without leadership. The nation was forced into unity with England in one commonwealth under Oliver Cromwell. Scotland was an occupied country once more, just as it had been in the days of Edward the Hammer, with English garrisons to hold the castles and English officials to conduct the affairs of state and justice. Lieutenant-General George Monck of Devon was appointed to be governor under Lord Protector Cromwell.

Scotland Under Cromwell

The Scots were also given the *same* trading rights as the English and 'all the privileges of a free people.' But trading rights that suited England often worked against Scotland's interests. Now Scots were banned from exporting wool and hides because the English had none to export, and their coal shipments were cut. At home cheap goods were brought into the country from England to push aside home products. Manufacturers went out of business and jobs were lost. Abroad they had the right now to trade with English colonies but war and storm had left the Scots with too few ships to carry their goods.

In return for 'all the privileges of a free people',

Portrait of Cromwell, the Lord Protector

the Scots were taxed more heavily than ever before. They were forced to pay for an army to keep out a King who had taxed them less severely. During the eight or so years that Cromwell and his army ruled the joint kingdoms, England grew strong and rich; Scotland remained too poor to benefit from the opportunities that the Protector's peace and justice had offered. Trade was dead and English wars with Holland lost for Scotland her best customer. Great families were broken, burgesses and their burghs no longer prospered and all sections of the people suffered. It was a hard time and Scotland was by Cromwell's own words 'a very ruined nation'. But not all was bad for Scotland. The common folk had always been ruled and oppressed by someone – at least under the Protectorate they had peace, law and order.

Charles II

Portrait miniature of Charles II

On 19th June 1660, Edinburgh shook to the great voice of Mons Meg as it boomed out from the castle's half moon battery in a mighty salute. The ringing of bells and the blare of fanfares, the crackle of fireworks and the beat of drums called the city to celebration. Wine ran freely at Mercat Cross. Scotland had news of its King once more. Charles II had returned. But more importantly, Scotland would be free again, free of English soldiers and English rulers. Or so it seemed. However it was not to Scotland that Charles returned, but England. In the twenty-five years of his reign he would never once cross the border. The kingdom in the north would be governed by royal decree from a desk in the south and as before, when his father was king, this distant rule would bring trouble to an already troubled land. It was not that Charles had come back seeking revenge for the death of his father, nor did he have strong ideas about religion that he wished to impose on Scotland. He was a Stuart and so knew the Scots. He was welcomed. But the trouble lay in Scotland itself; in its Church and in its poverty.

A Divided Church

The Church was divided against itself for there were still those who hung grimly to the Covenants. They demanded not only a Presbyterian Church for Scotland but for England too, and that it should be enforced on all. This they declared was no more than the Solemn League and Covenant had demanded. The King had signed the Covenant and must now honour it. This was the same stern face of the Covenanters that had driven Montrose from their numbers.

For the Covenanters, celebration and joy turned soon enough to disappointment at Charles II's lukewarm response to their demands. Disappointment became alarm when, in January 1661, he summoned his Parliament in Edinburgh and cancelled all the Acts that had been passed since 1633. Suddenly it was as if there had never been a National Covenant, never been a Great Rebellion. All that had been fought for and won was now at risk. Worse was yet to come.

The Plan for the Church of Scotland

With twenty-eight years of law-making now wiped out, Parliament faced a huge task. Led by the King's Commissioner, John Middleton, a great torrent of 393 new Acts poured out in six months. In the summer of 1662, the King now head of the Church once more, decided to bring back the bishops. In truth, it was a mild type of episcopal Church he planned with presbyteries and kirk sessions still completely in charge of local affairs. Because the General Assembly had not met for almost twenty years and would certainly have broken up in disorder had it done so, Charles now arranged for bishops to take its place under the control of Parliament. And Parliament was under the King.

The Conventicles

There was little to provoke in the King's plans for the Church of Scotland; there were no Books of Common Prayer nor Articles of Perth. But many were outraged. Three hundred ministers, mostly in the south-west, left their pulpits and gave up their livelihoods, refusing to accept this new episcopal order. In the fields and hills of Scotland a new sight was seen, and carried on the wind, a new sound was heard. Crowds of common folk gathered under open skies to pray, to sing psalms, and to hear the Holy Word from their 'outed' ministers. These outdoor services were called Conventicles, and in this manner Presbyterian preaching continued. The King and his bishops were defied.

The Earl of Rothes

Yet Charles meant to have his way. He replaced Middleton with the Earl of Rothes as his High Commissioner. Heavy fines were now imposed on all who failed to attend their Parish Church. Harmless as they were at first, the conventicles were made illegal and scattered at sabre-point by mounted troops wherever they were found.

But the covenanters were determined people and the conventicles went on. A King who signed a covenant and then ignored it would himself be ignored. Armed attack was met by armed resistance. The conventicles in their open mountain churches became armed bands, with sentries posted, ears and eyes strained for the sudden swoop by sabre-swinging dragoons.

A Conventicle meeting

Rullion Green

In November 1666 open revolt broke out in Galloway. The commonfolk rose against their tormentors and captured Sir James Turner, commander of the King's men in the area of Dumfries. He was unharmed. Through Ayrshire and Lanarkshire and on towards Edinburgh they marched with too few weapons and under too many banners and slogans from old campaigns. They sang the psalms and were led by a Wallace. They had more reckless courage than military skill. More left their ranks than joined them, for not all Scotland shared their anger, and they were easily enough put down. In the dusk of a late November evening they were scattered by the slashing charges of Sir Thomas Dalziel's dragoons at Rullion Green, not two miles north-west of Penicuick. Of the hundred or so taken, those who stood by the covenant died by the rope, many before the doors of their homes, some having first been tortured. Others who repented were 'mercifully' banished to slavery in distant Barbados. It seemed a brutal way to bring men and women to a liking for bishops and to a respect for the King as Head of the Church.

Gentler Measures

But it was not successful, this bitter rule of Rothes. As always, cruel oppression brought violent resistance and the nation bled. There were times of relief when the government softened its fierce policy. The Duke of Lauderdale who now replaced Rothes as Commissioner, offered the 'outed' ministers their pulpits once

Greyfriars Churchyard, Edinburgh

more, if they would only be loyal to the King. He didn't even demand that they should give up their covenant. Some gratefully accepted but others hardened their resistance. They still believed that all worship should be presbyterian and they could accept no less. Given the chance they too would have been oppressors, refusing even the freedom of worship to others that the government offered them. By 1673 harsher laws were being enforced once more. Now masters were to be fined if their servants did not attend church or if they failed to keep the King's peace and obey the Law. Preaching at open air conventicles was punishable by death.

Drumclog

But still the conventicles grew larger. In 1678 a host of Highlandmen were turned loose in the south-west, either to bring the rebel covenanters to order, or to provoke an open revolt which could more easily be crushed by government forces. The people were enraged by the looting and plunder of these wild men of the north, but it was the brutal murder, by the covenanters themselves, of the hated Archbishop James Sharp of St Andrews that lit the fuse of rebellion. The killers rode south and to the west where on the 1st June 1679, they joined a great conventicle at Drumclog, to the north of Loudoun Hill. Here Bruce had won his first battle. It was to be the first victory for the Covenanters too. This time when John Graham of Claverhouse, led the dragoons' charge it was stubborn armed men who turned from their prayers and drove them from the field; men who, in the name of the Lord, shot the prisoners they took.

A Swift Response

The King's revenge was swift. Within a month, at Bothwell Bridge on the River Clyde the covenant army, five thousand strong but ill-trained and quarrelsome, was crushed by the Duke of Monmouth. More than a thousand prisoners were marched two by two, to Edinburgh. They were held in Greyfriars churchyard in which they had first signed the National Covenant. For almost half a year they remained there without shelter, ill-fed and half-clad.

Most submitted to the King and promised not to bear arms. They were released. Two ministers were hanged in Edinburgh and others at Magus Muir, two miles from St Andrews where Archbishop Sharp met his cruel death. The remainder were shipped off for slavery in West Indian plantations but perished when their ship went down off Orkney with the wretched prisoners battened down below hatches.

James, Duke of York

The gentler touch of Monmouth who had ordered the release of those who promised not to take up arms again, was soon replaced by the iron fist when James, Duke of York, the King's brother came North. He had become a Roman Catholic in 1668 to the fury of the English Whigs who wanted to exclude him from the succession. Charles thought he would do less damage in Edinburgh than in Whitehall. Fewer now held true to their covenant but those who did, became even more fiercely defiant. Led by a wild young preacher called Richard Cameron, they openly disowned the King by a public declaration made at Sanquhar in Dumfriesshire on the 22nd June 1680.

The Cameronians

Cameron and his wild-eyed band styled themselves the 'Society Folk' and declared that they alone were the true Presbyterian Church of Scotland. Others gave them the name which would live on for three hundred

A group reads James Renwick's *Apologetical Declaration*

years – the 'Cameronians' – but did not share their mad certainty of God-given rightness. The Government outlawed them and any who helped them. They could be shot on sight. Exactly one summer month after their public treason in Sanquhar the Cameronians were brought to battle and routed by the King's dragoons at Aird's Moss near Auchinleck in Ayrshire. Richard Cameron himself was cut down. But the Cameronians went on. Donald Carghill now led them for a year during which, at the Torwood Conventicle, he formally 'excommunicated' the Duke of York and the Duke of Monmouth, the Lord Advocate Sir George Mackenzie, the brutal General Tam Dalziel, and even the King himself. Carghill was hanged in May 1681, and with his death the conventicles almost stopped. A month or so later Charles II appointed his brother James, Duke of York to be High Commissioner of Scotland.

But the Cameronians were not finished yet. In 1684 James Renwick roused their spirits with his defiant warning called the 'Apologetical Declaration' which he posted on the doors of churches and on market crosses throughout the south-west. It threatened death to anyone whom the Cameronians thought might decide to kill them. It was a wild 'kill or be killed' kind of policy. They were a determined and desperate people ready to use cruelties as great as any used against them and all was done in the name of Christ, their gentle and merciful Saviour.

The Duke of York's reply to Renwick's warning was swift and fierce. Anybody who supported this wild declaration was to be shot where he stood. Those who would give up the declaration were to be sent to Edinburgh to face trial. To the Cameronians it was a choice between the 'Bluidy Clavers', Commander of the King's dragoons, and the 'Bluidy Mackenzie', Chief Justice of the King's Court in Edinburgh, and both would bring them to the same end. In fact, only ten died on the orders of John Graham of Claverhouse and neither he nor Sir George Mackenzie were quite the monsters the covenanters reported them to be. They were ruthless men keeping cruel laws in a hard age. But execution without trial is murder and the murder stains the memory of John Graham, later to be remembered as 'Bonnie Dundee', just as the sack of Aberdeen had darkened the name of his famous ancestor, the great Montrose.

Death of Charles II

On the 6th February 1685, Charles II died and the Duke of York became King. Charles had prepared the way well for his brother. The throne was safe, the crown had great power and it was again possible for a Catholic to be King of Scotland.

Revolution

In Edinburgh on Tuesday, 10th February 1685, the Duke of York, brother of the dead King Charles II, was proclaimed James VII, King of Scots. There followed the usual show of excitement and celebration, but not with the usual warmth and joy. The King was a Catholic and he had refused to take the Coronation Oath to defend the Protestant religion. The nation, though ready to be loyal, was nervous.

An Act against the Covenanters

In Parliament, in April that year, a new Act against the Covenanters was passed. From now on it was treason to support the covenants, and an offence punishable by death to attend a conventicle. The few Cameronians remaining, harmless nuisances as they had become, were to be hunted down more brutally than before.

Rebellion

In May, the Earl of Argyll, son of Montrose's rival but not a covenanter, raised a feeble rebellion in the west. He had little help from the people who mostly were covenanters. It had been planned in support of the Duke of Monmouth's uprising in the south-west of England but Monmouth was late and his revolt just as feeble as Argyll's. The whole miserable affair collapsed almost before it had begun. The leaders were executed and their followers cruelly punished.

James had shown his royal strength. He now felt ready to tackle the Church. He was a headstrong man and proud, sure that as King he need answer to none but God. When Parliament advised against his changes in religion he chose to ignore its advice. When Parliament refused to do as he wished he swept it aside declaring that a monarch had 'no dependency on parliaments'. His father's fate had taught James very little.

Freedom of Worship

What the King wanted, and what he was determined to have, was freedom of worship for Catholics. He believed that it was his God-given duty to defend and advance the Catholic Church. With Parliament out of the way his Privy Council would do as he commanded. He made sure of this by replacing Protestant Lords (in

Portrait of James VII as the Duke of York

important government posts), with his own Catholic friends, and in 1687 'freedom of worship' was granted to all. Conventicles however, were still strictly against the law and there was no relief for the Cameronians who would still be miserably hounded.

And he went further. In Holyrood a Catholic chapel royal was set up once more; a Catholic school too, which would provide free education; and a printing press to publish Catholic information. People began to fear that freedom of worship would soon mean freedom to worship only as Catholics. They had already heard that the King's cousin, Louis XIV of France, was crushing the Huguenot Protestants there.

But freedom of worship meant something else too. It meant that Presbyterians could gather their strength once more. They could hold their services in meeting houses and preach to their flocks. People left Charles's Episcopal Church of Scotland and returned to their old preachers again; the words of the covenanters were heard once more.

The Scots, though they had been unhappy when Charles brought back the bishops, did not unite against them. Now that they were not forced by law to obey them, the bishops posed little threat. The Pope was a different matter. Most of the people feared and hated Rome. They would certainly unite against that. And of course James had lost the support of the ruling class by replacing his Protestant Lords with Catholics.

The common folk were angered by the Catholic changes they could see all around them. But still the King pushed on. On a bleak January day in 1688, James Renwick, leader of the Cameronians was taken prisoner in Edinburgh and sentenced to death. On the scaffold he sang the 103rd Psalm and declared, 'Lord, I die in the faith that Thou wilt not leave Scotland.'

Late 17th-century Scottish costume

If James knew the mood of his people he was too proud and too sure of his divine rightness to show it, or to show any respect for their feelings. The King's word was law and the nation grew more restless. With James Renwick dead the Cameronians now joined with the rest of the more peaceful Presbyterians to stiffen their ranks with new strength and courage. But still the King went on.

Birth of James Francis Edward Stuart

The last straw, when it came, was the birth of a baby. On Sunday, 10th June 1688, Mary of Modena, James'

Queen, bore the fifty-five year old King a son. Now the Catholic Stuarts line was secure. The people however, had had enough of it – at least the people in England, for it was there that the 'Glorious Revolution' began.

William of Orange

An urgent message was sent by leading men in England to Prince William of Orange in Holland. William was Viceroy of the Netherlands and James's son-in-law, married to his daughter Mary. Both were Protestants. Now William was invited to rule over Protestant England. On the 10th October 1688, before setting out, he sent a message to Scotland. He offered to remove the tyrant King James from there too, but the Scots were slow to accept. The Presbyterians were gaining in strength and felt more free to worship. They wanted to be sure that this William of Orange would grant them control of the Church of Scotland before they agreed to anything. And the bishops were uncertain too. James had been fairly friendly to their Episcopal Church. They were in no hurry to make up their minds either. Scotland remained tense and watchful.

William lands in Devon

In November 1688, the Dutchman's fleet had butted its wintry passage through the English Channel to find landfall, on Guy Fawkes' day, in the shelter of Tor Bay at Brixham on the east coast of Devon. William of Orange had arrived and with him came an army in three divisions. One was the Scots Brigade commanded by Hugh Mackay of Scourie on Sutherland's ragged western edge. And other Scots came too, exiled Covenanters returning once more to their homeland.

The Glorious Revolution

In England the Revolution was called 'Glorious' because it was bloodless. James was allowed to flee to France on December 23rd. William marched into London to be offered the English crown, which he accepted in February 1689. England had once more a Protestant King and Queen, William and Mary.

Portraits of William and Mary

But in Scotland things were different. Nothing really happened until James was in France and William in London. Then the storm broke. Edinburgh suddenly filled with great crowds who supported William, ready to fight if called upon. A mob rose in angry riot to tear apart the Catholic chapel royal at Holyrood and drive out the Catholic priests. In the south-west, on Christmas Day 1688, the Covenanters turned their pent up fury on James's curates, hurling them out of church and manse into the winter chill with neither food, shelter, nor hope of livelihood. More than two hundred suffered in this 'rabbling of the curates'.

Scotland was for a time without any proper government. The army had been called to England by James before he had decided to flee rather than fight. Mob and riot put law and order at risk, and the Scots now turned to England's new King for help. Even then William was not offered the throne. More than one hundred nobles and leading citizens sent a request that he should take over the nation's affairs until a choice of ruler could be made.

The Convention of Estates

On the 14th March 1689, a Scottish Parliament, summoned by William III of England, met in Edinburgh. Because there was no Scottish king it was called a Convention of Estates, a meeting of men of rank, men of God and men of business. Now it would be decided who should wear the crown.

The Convention was divided between those who wanted to have William as King – the Williamites; and those who still supported the Catholic King James VII (and II of England) – the Jacobites. And though there were more Williamites than Jacobites in Parliament Hall and throughout Edinburgh that day, they were outnumbered in the whole nation. More than that, the assembly sat under the menacing guns of Edinburgh Castle's Half-Moon Battery, still held for the Jacobites by the Catholic Duke of Gordon.

Hamilton elected President of the Convention

After a great deal of argument a rather shifty Duke of Hamilton, a Williamite of sorts, was narrowly elected to be President of the Convention over the equally shifty Marquis of Atholl. He had become a Jacobite of sorts only when William had overlooked him and chosen Hamilton as his man in Scotland.

Royal claims

Two days after the Convention opened, letters of application for the position of King of Scots were read to the assembly. William's came first, a quiet letter which brought little joy but no despair. The Dutchman made it clear that he would defend the Protestant faith. He wisely said nothing about how he would do it. Three regiments of the Scots Brigade under Mackay of Scourie came with the letter to help the Lords of Convention see its good sense. Now it was the Jacobite's turn. Now would be heard the words of the lawful King of Scotland.

'Bonnie Dundee'

Apart from Gordon's mighty guns, only the sixty horsemen of John Graham of Claverhouse, now Viscount Dundee, were there in support of James's claim. It was an angry bullying letter that the proud and headstrong King of Scots had written. He commanded loyalty from all, and threatened those who failed him. Such loyalty could mean having to share the Catholic King's Catholic religion. As the letter was read, most of his supporters in the Convention deserted him. Already the Marquis of Atholl was losing his taste for the Jacobite cause and its leadership was now in the hands of 'Bonnie Dundee'.

Wisely, Dundee left Edinburgh, promising to keep the peace and waste no time in clearing the West Port to put distance between himself and the angry city. With his followers he rode north swiftly to his rugged tower house of Claypots overlooking the Firth

of Tay a mile or so north-west of Broughty Ferry. But his mind was not on peace.

In the Convention there remained no voice for James. His only supporters were a few silent bishops who rarely attended and were called 'the Kirk invisible' by Viscount Dundee. Then, on the 30th March, the Convention declared Dundee a rebel and forced him down the path of open revolt.

William is chosen

In the first days of April 1689, the Lords of Convention came to a decision. James VII had failed in his proper duty as King and thus had lost his right to the throne of Scotland. A week later on Friday 11th, they issued the Claim of Right and offered the Crown to William and Mary.

Portrait of Viscount Dundee

From 'The Claim of Right', 1689

Declaration of the Estates of the Kingdom of Scotland containing the Claim of Right, and the offer of the Crown to their Majesties King William and Queen Mary.

... Therefore the Estates of the Kingdom of Scotland, Find and Declare that King James the Seventh being a professed Papist, did assume the Regal power, and acted as King, without ever taking the oath required by law, and hath by the advice of evil and wicked counsellors, invaded the fundamental constitution of the Kingdom, and altered it from a legal limited Monarchy, to an arbitrary despotick (sic) Power, and hath exercised the same, to the subversion of the Protestant religion, and the violation of the laws and liberties of the Kingdom, inverting all the ends of Government whereby hath forefaulted the right to the Crown, and the throne is become vacant.

And whereas His Royal Highness, William then Prince of Orange, now King of England, whom it hath pleased the Almighty God to make the Glorious Instrument of delivering these Kingdoms

from Popery and arbitrary power, did, by the advice of several Lords and Gentlemen of this nation, at London for the time, call the Estates of the Kingdom to meet on the fourteenth of March last in order to such an Establishment as that the Religion, Laws and Liberties might not be again in danger of being subverted; and the saids Estates being now assembled, taking to their most serious consideration the best means for attaining the ends aforesaid, do in the first place, as their ancestors in the like cases have usually done, for the vindicating and

asserting their ancient rights and liberties, declare that by law of this Kingdom, no Papist can be King or Queen of this Realm, nor bear any office whatsoever therein; nor can any Protestant successor exercise the regal power, until He or She swear the Coronation Oath . . .

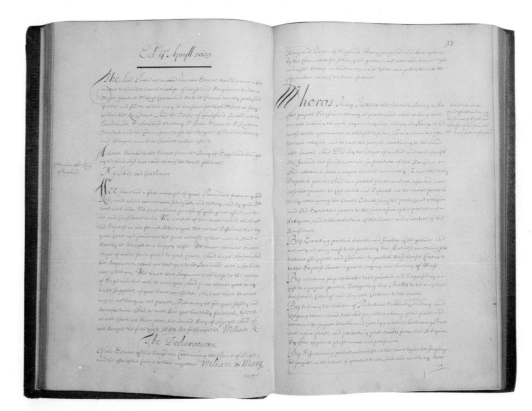

The Claim of Right, 1689

Scotland's Terms

It was quite a different offer from the one made to the Royal pair by England. It was tougher and more determined. In the past, kings had been too strong. Now by the Claim of Right they would be kept in their place. And there would be no more bishops. The Church of Scotland would be governed by the General Assembly, presbyteries and Kirk sessions. James VII had done wrong and had been put from his throne for it. The Convention in Scotland made this very clear. In England it was merely said that James had 'abdicated' or resigned his crown. The Scots also prepared a new Coronation Oath to make sure that William would be in no doubt of the new rules of kingship in the north. William was not pleased, but he would accept terms. On the 11th May 1689, William III of England became William II of Scotland, and Mary its Queen.

The Gathering of the Clans under James' standard

Dundee's Revolt

But trouble had already begun. Viscount Dundee had hoisted James's Standard outside his city. But support for James was poor. Dundee went north as Montrose had done and raised an army in the Highlands, an army of men interested in plunder and in putting down Clan Campbell. They cared little enough for the House of Stuart or the House of Orange, but they could fight.

By the bright water of the River Lochy, Bonnie Dundee planted his standard and called up his Highlanders from the west: from Clan Donald and Clan Cameron, the Stewarts too, and the MacLeans. They were about two thousand strong when they struck south and to the east from Lochaber, towards Atholl and the Lowlands beyond, where the road led to Perth and to Stirling. The news was rushed to Edinburgh that the fiery cross was being passed through the glens. Another Graham, perhaps another Montrose, was on the march.

To quench this rebel spirit of the Highland north, William's government sent General Hugh Mackay and more than four thousand men. Some were the seasoned troops of his Scots Brigade but mostly they were raw soldiers without battle practice.

Killiecrankie

Mackay learned that Castle Blair in Perthshire had been seized for King James by the Marquis of Atholl's own men when Atholl himself had rejoined William's cause. It was an important castle and Hugh Mackay planned to take it back from the Jacobites. He marched north on 27th July, by Tummel Water and Pitclochry into the deep grim Pass of Killiecrankie. Alongside the roaring flow of the River Garry, Mackay's four thousand threaded their way between the steep sides of the gorge. To the north, at the head of the gloomy pass, Bonnie Dundee and his clansmen held the high ground. They watched and waited.

As King William's General brought his troops out of the Pass of Killiecrankie, he wheeled them to bring their musket fire to bear on the Jacobite positions. Dundee's command unleashed all the wild fury of a screaming slashing Highland charge. Mackay's men had no time to screw on their clumsy bayonets before the clansmen were upon them and round them and over them; they fled in terror into the dark narrow pass there to be slaughtered in hundreds. The battle was over in minutes. The victory was Dundee's. General Mackay gathered together those survivors he could find and made a silent retreat south over the low hills of Atholl under the brief darkness of a midsummer night.

For Bonnie Dundee the day was won but, by a stray musket ball, his life was lost. He died at the very moment of his triumph. But news of his crushing victory brought panic to Edinburgh. The Privy Council made their plans for a hasty move south to England should the Jacobite Highlanders break through to Stirling.

But the grieving clansmen lost heart at the death of their leader. They never had been much interested in the cause of the Catholic King James. Dundee himself was a staunch Protestant. And though the Highlanders now marched south it was plunder and not loyalty to James that filled their minds.

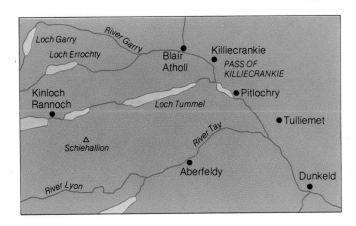

Dunkeld

The cathedral town of Dunkeld lay in the path of the advancing Highlanders and it was a prize worth taking. But its defence was in the tougher hands, a new regiment born out of the youngest and hottest of the Covenanters and called – the 'Cameronians'. It had just been formed in Edinburgh by the Duke of Argyll and now, twelve hundred strong, if stood to the defence of Dunkeld under its brave young commander, William Cleland.

Only months before these men had been outlaws, hunted down by the King's dragoons. The courage that had kept them during those dark days would be needed now to face the Highland charge when it came. And face it they did. With their commander shot dead in the first minutes of the battle and the huge weight of the Highland advance driving them back, they dug in their heels and fought and fought. Amongst the smoke and din of the bitter struggle they held their ground and then, inch by inch, pressed forward.

In the face of such stubborn courage and fierce assault the clans lost all taste for the prize and withdrew to their Highland glens once more. The Cameronians had won. James's cause was lost. The psalms the young regiment sang that day in the streets of Dunkeld were loud in praise of a first battle won, and of a revolution saved.

Engraving of the valley and town of Dunkeld, from John Slezer's *Theatrum Scotiae*

Worksection

Understand Your Work
The Return of the King

Scotland Under Cromwell
1 Who ruled Scotland and England in 1652?
2 Who was his governor in Scotland?
3 What advantage was Scotland meant to have in the new Commonwealth?
4 How did this work against the Scottish interests?
5 Why were English goods preferred to Scottish ones?
6 Which country did better under Cromwell, Scotland or England?
7 What benefit did the common folk have in Scotland?

Charles II and the Church
1 When did Charles II return to his kingdom?
2 Did he ever come to Scotland?
3 How did he govern Scotland?
4 What caused the trouble in Charles II's reign?
5 What did the Covenanters demand?
6 What did Charles do in January 1661 which upset many Scots?
7 Who introduced the King's new laws for the Scottish Church?
8 Should the new laws have upset the Scots?
9 What were the main changes that caused the trouble?

The Conventicles
1 Where did most of the ministers come from who objected to the new rules?
2 What did they do when they were not allowed to preach in their own way in their own pulpits?
3 What were these meetings called?
4 How were the ministers who preached there described?
5 How did the King, Charles II, attempt to stop the unlawful church services?
6 Who led the King's attack on the Conventicles?
7 What happened when a Conventicle was discovered?
8 How did the Covenanters resist the King's efforts?

Revolution

The New King and the Church
1 Why were the Scots not keen on James VII as their King?
2 How did James behave when Parliament was opposed to his ideas?
3 What was it that he had not learned any lessons from?
4 How did he want Catholics in Scotland treated?
5 Why did this trouble the people?
6 How did freedom of worship help the Presbyterians?
7 What finally brought about the Glorious Revolution?
8 Where did William of Orange first rule?

The Glorious Revolution
1 Why was the revolution in England called 'glorious'?
2 What happened in February 1689?
3 How were Catholic priests treated in south-west Scotland?
4 What was the Convention of Estates?
5 What difference was there between the letters of William and James?
6 Why did Viscount Dundee leave Edinburgh in a hurry?
7 Who were 'the Kirk invisible'?
8 When was the Scottish crown offered to William of Orange?
9 How did the Scottish offer differ from the one made by England?

Dundee's Revolt
1 Where did Dundee raise his army?
2 Who marched against Viscount Dundee?
3 Where did the two forces meet?
4 What was William's general planning to do?
5 What were the results of the battle?
6 What was Viscount Dundee's own religion?
7 Who defended Dunkeld against the Highland force?
8 What was the result of the defeat of the Highlanders at Dunkeld?

Use Your Imagination

1 How do you suppose the important people in Scotland felt about the way things were in 1652?

2 How do you imagine the common folk felt?

3 Do you think the King was wise to try to crush the Covenanters by force?

4 What do you think King Charles II might have done to avoid trouble with the Covenanters?

5 Do you think there were lessons that James VII could have learned from Mary Queen of Scots' experience when she came to the thone?

6 How would you have advised James VII to behave when he became King?

7 Why was the nation becoming more and more restless under King James VII?

8 Why do you think the birth of an heir to James VII is described on page 9 as the last straw?

9 Why do you suppose 'Scotland remained tense and watchful' after the arrival of King William in England?

10 Why do you think Viscount Dundee promised to keep the peace as he left Edinburgh in 1689?

Further Work

1 Here is a description of a cook in an Edinburgh tavern around 1730:

'The cook was too filthy an object to be described; only another English gentleman whispered to me and said, he believed, if the fellow were to be thrown against the wall, he would stick to it.

   Twisting round his hand a greasy towel, he stood waiting to know what we would have for supper.'
Letters from the North of Scotland Capt. Bart

Now try to see this cook in your imagination and then add some sentences to the first paragraph, describing his hair, face, hands, dress, manner of speech and so on. Make him the dirtiest, scruffiest cook in the world!

2 This is how the Battle of Killiecrankie was described by an old Highlander to Capt. Bart:

'He told me that Mackay extended his line, which was only two deep, the whole length of the plain; designing, as he supposed, to surround the Highlanders . . . That after the first firing, the Rebels came down, six or seven deep, to attack the King's (William's) troops; . . . they, by their weight charged through, through those feeble files; and made with their broad-swords a most carnel carnage and many others who expected no quarter, in order to escape the Highland fury, threw themselves into that rapid river (the Garry), and were drowned.'
Letters from the North of Scotland

Try to visit the Pass of Killiecrankie where you will learn more about the battle.

3 There is a song and pipe tune called '*Bonnie Dundee*' which tells of the Viscount's efforts in the revolution. Try to find a copy to read or sing in your class.

4 Imagine that you are attending a Conventicle but you and some friends have wandered off some considerable distance. Suddenly you hear approaching horsemen. You must warn the Covenanters that the King's Dragoons are coming but you cannot get back before the horsemen. How can you trick the King's men? Discuss this in your group and see if you can invent a plan to delay the dragoons and save the Conventicle. When you have agreed how the plan will work and what part each of you will play, write your own account of what happened to you during the adventure.

   When you have finished your separate accounts then each of you can tell the others of your own experiences as though you were meeting again after the events of that exciting night.

One Parliament

Before John Graham, Viscount Dundee, had roused the clansmen to revolt, William's government had not thought enough about the Highlands. Now they thought a great deal. Though William was firmly on the Scottish Throne there still lingered a fear that rebellion might come again and if it did, that it would originate in the Western Highlands. There was always the chance that the clans would unite against Argyll and his hated Campbells.

Bribes for the Highlanders

In London plans were made to end the Highland threat. It was common enough then to manage affairs of state by bribery. Loyalty came when a pension was granted. Now the Government, with little enthusiasm from King William who thought loyalty from subjects should be automatic, tried to buy the support of the Highland clans. Twelve thousand pounds in all was offered. But it did not work. Some Chiefs refused to be bribed. Others were happy enough to take the money but still withheld their support.

An Oath of Loyalty

The Government now changed tactics. In the August of 1691 all the clans were instructed to swear loyalty to King William before New Year's Day 1692. Any who failed to do so would be punished to the utter limit of the law. But here there was a real problem for the clans. Their chiefs were torn between honour and good sense. They needed King James to release them from their solemn oath to him before they could properly swear loyalty to his Dutch son-in-law. It was a problem which suited those who dreamed up the scheme, for it meant that there would likely be clans who failed to meet the deadline. Then an example could and would be made of the latecomers and the savage Highlands would at last be still.

The clan chiefs sent urgent messages to King James in France for his advice; they waited anxiously for his reply. As late summer reddened to autumn, and autumn gave way before the hard edge of a northern winter they were still waiting. It was near the end of December when word at last came from James that the clans were free to look to their own safety. Most chiefs were able to take the oath just in time. To Sir John Dalrymple, Master of Stair and master too of this plan to divide the rebel north, it was disappointing news.

On Hogmanay 1691, a Highland chief, Alasdair MacDonald known as MacIan, was butting his way through a bitter blizzard to Fort William, to give his oath of loyalty. But MacIan's weary journey was in vain. The Sheriff was at Inveraray, eighty winter miles away. MacIan continued his journey in the bleak wind swept sleet. It was not until January 3rd that he arrived. His oath of loyalty was not taken until the 6th, when the Deputy Sheriff in Inveraray had recovered from his New Year celebrations.

A Plot against the Macdonalds

On the 11th January this welcome news reached Chief Secretary Dalrymple in London. The Chief of the Macdonalds had failed to meet the deadline; not the mighty MacDonalds of Keppoch or Glengarry, but MacIan of the smaller and wilder branch of the family, Clan MacDonald of lonely Glencoe.

It could not have suited the Master of Stair better. This was a clan with few friends and a bad reputation for robbing and trouble making. Few would regret very much what happened to them. An example could now be made. They would be 'rooted out and cut off.'

Glencoe

At the end of January, Captain Robert Campbell of Glenlyon led a regiment of Argyll's soldiers into Glencoe. For almost a fortnight they shared the food and shelter of the MacDonalds. Then in the winter dawn of Saturday, 13th February 1692, without warning they turned their swords against their hosts. Their helpless victims were butchered in bed or as they fled unclad and unarmed into the wild bleakness of Glencoe. MacIan and thirty-six of his clan, including several women and children, were murdered that miserable dawn. Others escaped the sword, pike and bayonet only to perish in the bitter cold of the high winter slopes.

There had been treachery in the Highlands in the past but this was different. This awful deed had been by order of the Government. The Massacre of Glencoe shocked and angered the people of Scotland and of many other countries. France first broke the news. Now William and his Government would no longer be trusted. And though the Master of Stair was disgraced and sacked from all government office, no real justice was done; no one was punished for the mass murder of the Macdonalds of Glencoe.

Glencoe

The Company of Scotland

While official enquiries were still being made into Glencoe, in 1695 a new project began to fire the minds of the Scottish people. King William had agreed to an Act passed by the Scottish Parliament setting up a national trading company called the Company of Scotland. Excitement ran high as plans went ahead for a great new venture. Soon Scotland would grow rich from trade with Africa, America and other foreign countries. This was the kind of dream to take men's minds off bleak Glencoe and the stark famine which racked the northern kingdom that year and the next when the harvest failed in the windswept rain of two miserable autumns.

The man with the dream was William Paterson of Dumfriesshire, Scottish founder of the Bank of England. His vision was of a great joint trading venture with England. So keen was he, and so confident, that hundreds of thousands of pounds poured in from both sides of the border. The Company of Scotland had most of the support it needed in a matter of weeks and hopes ran high.

The First Setback

Then fell the first blow. Business rivals in England were outraged by the new national company. They thought it might take profit from their own pockets. They protested long and loud in Parliament, and the English merchants, who had put up almost three hundred thousand pounds, were forced to withdraw. And worse than that, when the Scots turned to other countries for help, William again, with his English government, blocked their efforts.

But still the Company went on. Paterson's dream would yet come true. He had promised that 'trade will increase trade' and 'money will make money'. The Scots were determined. By a huge effort the massive sum of four hundred thousand pounds was raised in Scotland alone. It was almost as much as the coinage of the whole land was worth. It was more by far than the country could afford but spirits were high and the future looked bright.

The dream that dazzled all Scotland was of a great free port on the narrow land strip that joins South and North America. A port would be created on the Isthmus of Panama; a port where east meets west. There the wealth of Europe would be exchanged for the riches of the Orient. The profit and the glory would be Scotland's. It was to be 'the door of the seas, the key of the universe.'

The Darien Colony

The site chosen for the new port lay in a sheltered haven to be called the Bay of Caledonia, on the western margin of the Gulf of Uraba, better remembered in Scotland as the Gulf of Darien. Under a broad summer sky bright with hope, on 14th July 1698, five proud ships, lion banners flying, drew away from Leith harbourside and a cheering, waving, crying, laughing throng. On board were twelve hundred adventurers with their supplies and stores, with cargoes for trade, and with the dreams and prayers of a nation. They would plant a Scottish flag and build a Scottish colony in the distant Caribbean, in Darien, six thousand miles from their homeland.

But King William had not yet finished with his Scottish subjects and their plans for new trade. Now he struck at the Darien Scheme. Because he was busy with plans to keep peace in Europe he was anxious not to upset Spain. Unfortunately, the Spanish claimed Darien as their own. Now a Scottish expedition was on its way to set up a colony there. Spain protested and William, acting as King of England, ordered that English colonies in North America or the Caribbean were to give no help to his Scottish subjects. He wanted Spain to see that he had nothing to do with the Darien Scheme – even though it was he who had granted the Royal Charter to the Company of Scotland in the first place.

A First Failure

Had things gone well for the Scots in Panama, the royal interference might not have mattered too much. But they had no real experience of settling a colony and little knowledge of the place they had chosen for it. On the map it looked ideal; a neck of land narrow enough that a short overland route would readily connect the new port on the Atlantic shore with the open Pacific and the treasures of the East. What the map could not show was the breathless clinging heat of the day or the stifling warmth of airless nights, thick with fever laden mosquitoes. It told little of wet smothering jungle and steaming swamp, or of the endless pitiless tropical rain. The New Caledonia was an evil place for men, women and children born in the chilly windswept north. And they were unprepared and ill-provisioned.

The adventure became a disaster. Of those who survived the long, long sea crossing to make that first landfall in November, many died of disease and starvation in the sickly heat of Darien. The following July the exhausted survivors abandoned the colony to sail for Scotland. They left only deserted huts and lonely graves to mark their proud ambition. One only of their ships safely completed the homeward passage.

The Darien Colony in the Caribbean

'Isthmus of Darien' drawn in about 1699

The Second Expedition

Before news of the disaster reached Scotland, another expedition had already set sail. Four more ships had been bought and provisioned by a nation racked by famine and poverty but still high with hope. They too made a winter landfall one year after the first party. They rebuilt the settlements and tried not to be daunted by the four hundred graves that were scattered about them. Not only was there the weather and yellow fever to fight, now there were the Spaniards too. Sure that William would not help the Scots, the Spaniards tried to drive them from the new colony. Twice they struck and twice they were driven back into the jungle. But in March 1700, on the third attempt and only after enduring a bitter month of hopeless siege, the Scots surrendered with honour. Weary from fever and hunger, from wounds and exhaustion, the survivors boarded their ships and had to be helped by the Spaniards to raise the heavy anchors. Most would perish before sighting their homeland.

Of the two and a half thousand men, women and children who made the crossings to Panama only three hundred returned alive. Nine ships were lost, given up or destroyed and most of the money raised by the Company of Scotland was gone. It was a disaster as great as Flodden Field. Again the Scots blamed the English. King William would be remembered not for the Revolution but for Glencoe and Darien. The nation in the face of disaster, turned against its partner in the south; their anger had blinded the Scots to their own bad planning, bad equipping, and doubtful leadership of the wondrous scheme in Darien. All blame, they decided, was England's. There was rebellion in the air.

When news had first reached Edinburgh of the settlers early victories against the Spaniards, cheering mobs had smashed windows of those they suspected of supporting William's government. The bells of the Capital rang to the tune of 'Wilful Willie, wilt thou be wilful still?' When the Darien Scheme collapsed William had to face the anger of the Scottish Parliament and his excuses and promises did little to soothe their feelings or to quiet the people's fury.

Yet rebellion did not come. The Scots were divided amongst themselves. Most preferred William with all his faults, to the Catholic James VII, whom he had replaced.

Death of King William

It was on the 8th March 1702, in London, that William died after a riding accident. Now to the throne of the troubled realms came Anne Stuart, daughter of the exiled James VII (and II of England). She too was faced with the growing storm. A year earlier, the English Parliament had decided who should have the throne after Queen Anne if she had no heirs of her own. They did so without asking the Scots for their opinion. The throne they declared would pass to Sophia of Hanover, granddaughter of James VI (and I of England), and her heirs if Protestant. But Scotland would not be ignored. Instead, in 1704, came a defiant challenge. The English could have Sophia if they wished; Scotland would choose a monarch for herself. And they forced Queen Anne to accept this by refusing to vote her any supplies until she did. Scotland might again be a separate kingdom and then there could well be war.

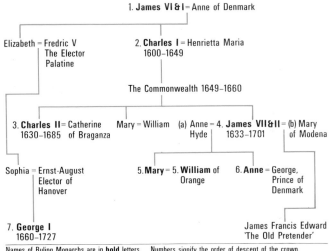

1. **James VI & I** = Anne of Denmark

Elizabeth = Fredric V
The Elector
Palatine

2. **Charles I** = Henrietta Maria
1600–1649

The Commonwealth 1649–1660

3. **Charles II** = Catherine
1630–1685 of Braganza

Mary = William

(a) Anne = 4. **James VII & II** = (b) Mary
Hyde 1633–1701 of Modena

Sophia = Ernst-August
Elector of
Hanover

5. **Mary** = 5. **William** of
Orange

6. **Anne** = George,
Prince of
Denmark

7. **George I**
1660–1727

James Francis Edward
'The Old Pretender'

Names of Ruling Monarchs are in **bold** letters.   Numbers signify the order of descent of the crown.

English Threats

Early in 1705 the Westminster Parliament struck back. The English threatened to ban all imports of Scottish cattle, coal and linen from Christmas Day that year until the Scots agreed to England's choice of ruler. The mood between the countries grew darker and the shadow of approaching war ever longer. A Scottish merchant ship belonging to the Company of Scotland was seized by the English in the River Thames and held against all demands for her release. And worse, an English merchantman was arrested in the Forth by the Scots and her captain with two of his officers were put on trial for imagined piracy. They were found guilty and hanged because of the mob's fevered anger and because they were English. Captain Green, his mate Mader and his gunner Simson were no pirates but not even Queen Anne could save them.

By now England was at war with France and could not face Scotland too. Scotland, though roused to a fury, was suffering desperately from trading failure and the Darien disaster. The Scots could simply not afford to be cut off from trade with England. War would be a calamity.

A Search for Peace

If there could not be war then the two countries would have to find their way to peace. William had known this in 1702 when he sent from his deathbed an urgent appeal to his Parliament at Westminster, pleading that 'nothing can contribute more to the present and future peace, security and, happiness of England and Scotland than a firm and entire union.' Queen Anne knew this too when, at the beginning of her reign, she invited the same Parliament 'to consider of proper methods towards attaining a Union with Scotland.'

Now Scotland too, suffering in its own pitiful poverty and faced with England's bullying threat to cut off trade, had to still its fury and quieten its pride. At Parliament Hall in Edinburgh the Secretary of State warned, 'We are utterly ruined should these laws take effect.' But not all present agreed and for almost a month the debate raged until, at last, it was decided to unite with England. There would be but one Parliament as well as one monarch to govern the united kingdom of Great Britain. England withdrew its threat against Scottish imports.

The Union

On 16th April 1706, commissioners from each nation met separately at Westminster. For two months, and only in writing, they argued and bargained before the terms on which the two Parliaments would be joined were agreed. The Scots would have equal trading rights with England and the sum of four hundred thousand pounds sterling, partly to make up for the losses suffered in Darien and partly for new expenses the country would face. They would keep their own Scotish Law and Law Courts. England would have her choice of Sophia of Hanover and her Protestant heirs, to follow Anne to a British throne and much more too. In Parliament there would be one hundred and ninety English lords and only sixteen from Scotland; five hundred and thirteen English and Welsh commoners and only forty-five from Scotland. Only English weights and measures would be used and there would be a new common money system. And for the whole United Kingdom there would be one Great Seal and one flag on which would be joined together the crosses of St Andrew and St George.

The Treaty of Union, 1706

But now when I consider this treaty, as it hath been explained and spoke to before us this three weeks past, I see the English constitution remaining firm, the same two houses of Parliament, the same taxes, the same customs, the same excises, the same trading companies, the same municipal laws and courts of judicature: and all ours either subjected to regulations or annihilations: only we have the honour to pay their old debts, and to have some few persons present for witness to the validity of the deed, when they are pleased to contract more. Good God! What, is this an entire surrender?

Lord Belhaven in the Scottish Parliament,
4th November, 1706

A Stormy Passage

These were the terms with which the commissioners now returned to their own Parliaments. On 12th October 1706, they were presented to the Scots Parliament and at once there was nationwide anger and protest. In Edinburgh, in Glasgow and in Dumfries mobs took to the streets. For three long months Parliament debated, one by one, the twenty-five terms. For three long months the nation was in uproar. Everywhere riot exploded. Nowhere could anyone, whatever their religion or politics, agree with all the terms. English troops marched to the border ready to cross if called upon. Scottish troops shared the nation's unrest and were not to be trusted. Copies of the treaty were being burnt in market places and men called for rebellion.

In Parliament the heat was just as fierce. Lord Belhaven called it the murder of one's native land and roared out 'Good God! What! Is this an entire surrender?' But slowly and painfully each of the terms was confirmed and on Wednesday, 19th March 1707, James Douglas, Duke of Queensberry, High Commissioner to the Queen, rose to declare,

> 'My Lords and Gentlemen, it is a great satisfaction to the Queen that Union is thus happily concluded in Her Reign and I am commanded by Her Majesty to assure you, that nothing shall be omitted on Her part, to make the whole Island feel the good effects of it.'

The Duke of Queensbury presenting the treaty to Queen Anne

He spoke again on Tuesday, 25th March, when the angry voices were quietened, the furious debate stilled.

> 'My Lords and Gentlemen, the Public Business of this session being now over, it is full time to put an end to it.'

The last Scottish Parliament

It was an end to that and all sessions, for the Scottish Parliament would never meet again. Four hundred years of brave and bitter struggle for independence now ceased. And yet, though poverty and starvation had brought the northern kingdom to join with its neighbour in the south, in one British nation under one British flag, the Scots in their hearts would remain Scottish.

On 1st May 1707, the two nations became one and on Thursday, 23rd October that same year, the first ever Parliament of Great Britain met at Westminster. A new nation was born.

Worksection

One Parliament
Understand Your Work

Bribes, Oaths and Plots

1 What was it that the British Government feared after William came to the throne?
2 How did the government first try to end the threat?
3 Why did the plan not work?
4 What new plan was tried?
5 What problem was there for the Highland Clans in the new plan?
6 What did the government planners hope would happen?
7 What caused MacIan of the MacDonalds to be late with the clan's oath of loyalty?
8 Who was pleased to hear of the late oath?
9 Why was he particularly pleased that it was a small weak clan?

Glencoe

1 Who led the Argyll soldiers into Glencoe?
2 Did they attack the MacDonalds at once?
3 How was the massacre carried out?
4 What happened to many who escaped the sword?
5 Why was the treachery thought to be doubly bad?
6 How did the people at home and abroad feel about what King William and his government had done?

The Company of Scotland

1 What was it that excited Scotland in 1695?
2 Why was Scotland in desperate need of good news at this time?
3 Who was behind the new scheme?
4 What other enterprise was he later responsible for?
5 Who were upset by the Company of Scotland?
6 What happened because of their objections?
7 How much money was raised in Scotland alone?
8 What was Paterson's plan for the Company of Scotland?

The Darien Colony and first failure

1 Where was the Darien Colony set up?
2 When did the expedition to found it set out?
3 What did King William do now?
4 Why did he hinder his Scottish subjects in this way?
5 In what way was he being dishonest?
6 Was it King William's interference alone which caused trouble for the settlers?
7 What conditions caused illness among the Scots in Darien?
8 How long did they remain there?

The Second Expedition

1 Why did a second expedition set sail after the first had been such a disaster?
2 What did they try not to be worried by when they reached Darien?
3 What added problem did this expedition have to face?
4 When did they finally abandon the colony?
5 How many people died in the two expeditions to Darien?
6 What would King William be remembered for by many Scots?
7 Why could the Scots not see the faults in their own planning of the expeditions?
8 Why did rebellion not come?

Death of King William

1 How long did King William reign over Britain?
2 Who was his successor?
3 What caused trouble between Scotland and England?
4 How did the Scots get their way?
5 What might this have led to?
6 How did the Westminister Parliament strike back?
7 What unjust action took place against an English merchant ship and her crew?
8 Why could the Scots not afford to be without English trade?

A Search for Peace and Union

1 How did King William believe peace between Scotland and England could be found?
2 What was Queen Anne's view on this?
3 Why did England withdraw its threat to cut off trade?
4 When did negotiations to bring about the Union begin?
5 How were they conducted?
6 What money would Scotland receive?
7 How would parliament be made up?
8 Who thought the terms to be 'an entire surrender'?

A Stormy Passage

1 How did the Scots feel about the terms for the Union?
2 How long did it take to agree the twenty-five terms?
3 Why were the English troops put on alert?
4 Why were Scottish troops not used?
5 When was the last ever meeting of the Scottish Parliament?
6 On what date did the two nations become one?
7 When and where did the first Parliament of Great Britain meet?

Use Your Imagination

1 What do you think was the real purpose behind the *very short time* allowed to the clans in which to swear their loyalty?

2 Do you feel the government were acting justly when they decided that Clan MacDonald was being disloyal because their oath was late?

3 Why do you think no one was properly punished for the Massacre of Glencoe?

4 What was the condition of the Scottish people in 1695?

5 Do you think those English businessmen who complained about the Company of Scotland were objecting just because it was Scots who would make the profit?

6 What do you suppose William Paterson meant when he said that 'trade will increase trade' and 'money will make money'?

7 Look at a globe of the world and see if you can tell what was meant when Darien was described as 'the door of the seas, the key of the universe'?

8 How might the Scots have planned better for the Darien Scheme?

9 What do you think was meant by 'Wilful Willie wilt thou be wilful still'?

10 What do you think the English thought of their new partners, and led them to imagine that they could decide the heir to the throne without consulting the Scots?

11 What do you suppose made some Scots accept that Union with their old enemy was a good idea?

Further Work

1 Imagine yourself a child of the MacDonalds of Glencoe that wintry dawn almost three hundred years ago. Something disturbs your sleep and you see shadowy figures moving in the grey light. You know there is danger, you must warn all your family . . . What do you do? What happens? Write the story of that fateful morning. Call it '*Massacre*' or '*Escape*' or something you choose yourself.

2 The book '*Glencoe*' by John Prebble tells about the massacre in a story-like way. Try to find a copy in the library so that you can enjoy reading the vivid descriptions.

3 Here is a poem to read and enjoy. It is called '*The Far Farers*' and pictures a scene like the one at Leith when the ships left on their long voyage to distant Darien.

> The broad sun,
> The bright day,
> White sails,
> On the blue bay:
> The far-farers
> Draw away,
> Light the Fires
> And close the door.
> To the old homes,
> To the loved shore,
> The far-farers
> Return no more.

You could use this poem as a model for a poem of your own about the homecoming of the Darien survivors. Study each line of the poem and write one to match it – but from the point of view of a returning survivor.

4 Discuss in your group what steps might have been taken in the planning of the Darien Scheme that would have made it more likely to succeed. Think about these questions as you do so:

a What would you need to know in order to plan properly?

b How might you find out?

c What special equipment and supplies would you take?

d What specially trained personnel would you require?

Make a note of your group ideas under the heading – *Advice to the Company of Scotland*.

The Last of the Royal Stuarts

In the north and in the south of the new kingdom of the British, those men who had struggled to bring about the Union, strove to make it last. For many Scots it promised a better life. Those who were against it, and there were many, now plotted to end it.

From 1707, each new year brought to more and more Scots reasons to regret the Union. For more than a quarter century it looked like yet another disaster for Scotland. It was a bitter awakening from dreams of richer trade and an end to poverty and famine; dreams of a friendly south and no more wasting war; dreams which had made bearable the surrender of nationhood.

The Union under stress

Instead, Scottish trade now became even worse than before. Just as when the Lord Protector Cromwell had made trade 'free' between the countries, English goods of equal quality but cheaper, again flooded over the border. Home products were driven off the market and their makers out of business. Richer stronger industries from the south swamped those in Scotland. The British government, who were almost all Englishmen, neither understood the problems of the north nor cared about Scotland's hardship.

Wild and haughty claims were made which would deeply hurt the Union. When Scottish members of Parliament protested that Scotland's very important linen making should be treated in the same way as the great woollen industry of England and not be made to suffer heavy export taxes, they were asked by the Lord Treasurer, 'Have we not bought the Scots, and a right to tax them?' It seemed that important Englishmen thought the £400,000 compensation agreed in the treaty was the price of Scotland. And when the Scots denied this way of understanding the Act of Union they were told, 'Whatever are or may be the laws of Scotland, yet she now is subject to the sovereignty of England, she must be governed by English laws and maxims.'

'Entire surrender'

It seemed to be Edward I all over again. Englishmen still thought that they should rule the north. To many Scots the Union had become 'entire surrender' as it had been called by Lord Belhaven. Wherever Scotland turned the route was closed. A scheme to build roads into the Highlands and bring out the timber of the great forests there was turned down, and imports from American colonies and Norway preferred. A tax on salt almost broke the Scottish herring fisheries, and English but not Scottish coal could now be exported tax free to Ireland.

The Scots were also called upon to fight and die in other peoples' wars in other peoples' lands. Scots blood ran in Flanders where the Cameronians fought stubbornly through dreadful losses, under the great English general, John Churchill, Duke of Marlborough for the glory of the new Great Britain. The Scots Greys and the Fusiliers were there too leading and falling in Marlborough's famous victories. Of one family in Ayrshire five sons served and four died in distant foreign fields, and there seemed little that was glorious about that. Though they fought bravely for their new nation, the Scots were given little say on deciding whether there should be war or peace with France and their anger grew.

The fighting Cameronians

Jacobite Hopes

In all this unhappiness with the Union, one body of people saw hope – the Jacobites. Though James VII was dead, there was still his son James, half-brother to Queen Anne, another Stuart to wear the British crown. King Louis XIV of France saw that Scotland was weakly defended, her best troops serving with Marlborough in France. Within a year of the Union he had sent a fleet under Admiral Forbin with a force of five thousand and a new King James VIII to claim the throne of the United Kingdom. Bad weather, mistakes and Admiral Byng with twenty-six men-of-war persuaded them not to land. It was close, but the Union had survived its first direct attack. Most Scots breathed again. The haughty English were preferred to a Catholic James. If the Union was to end it would not be to put another Catholic on the Scottish throne.

Portrait of James Francis Edward Stuart

A Motion in the Lords

By 1713 the Union was again under attack. This time in the House of Lords. On the 2nd June, Earl Findlater rose to complain of the heavy taxes and ruin of trade, the removal of the Privy Council and law changes Scotland had suffered. When he called for a vote against the Union he was defeated by only four votes. Once more the Union just survived. When it was challenged again it would be by the Jacobite sword.

King George I

On Sunday, 1st August 1714, Queen Anne, the last of the Stuarts to wear the crown, died. A German George I, son of Sophia of Hanover, now came to the British throne. There was no immediate trouble, but the new King soon chose to upset a number of Scottish nobles. Exactly a year after Anne's death, John Erskine, Earl of Mar, called Bobbing John for the speed with which

Portrait of the Earl of Mar

he changed sides, left London still stinging from the King's latest rebuke and made his way north by sea. He had had enough of George I. Now he would be a Jacobite. He landed at Elie in the Firth of Forth and began at once to rouse the Jacobites. His urgent riders hurried secret messages throughout Scotland.

The 'Fifteen

Five weeks later, amid a gathering of six hundred at Castleton of Braemar in Aberdeenshire, the Royal Standard of the Stuarts was raised in the name of King James VIII of Scotland. Mar called for all good men to fight 'for the relief of our country from oppression and a foreign yoke too heavy for us ... to bear'. The Mackintoshes were there and the MacDonalds of Keppoch, the Clansmen of Glencoe with the followers of Chief Glenlyon who had arranged that bleak and bitter massacre. All had quarrels amongst themselves but all hated the Union more. They expected help from France and news soon of an uprising in the south of England. They hoped to gain the support of all who had wearied of the Union.

But it was a dithering kind of rebellion. The Jacobites seized Perth and Inverness but got no French help and no English news. And though ten thousand men had come to his standard, Mar stayed in the Highlands until October, while the Duke of Argyll held the Carse of Stirling for the government with less than half that strength. There he defended the Jacobite route to the lowlands. Bobbing John was no Montrose. He watched nervously from the Highlands unsure of himself and his army. When at last the strike south came it was with only two thousand men and under William Mackintosh of Borlum, a crusty old soldier of skill and experience.

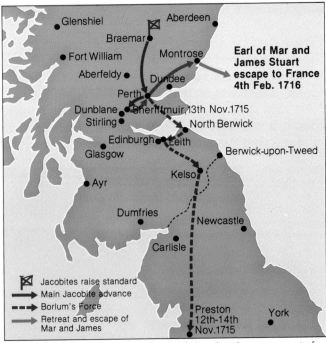

Map of Scotland and northern England showing the movement of the armies during the '15'

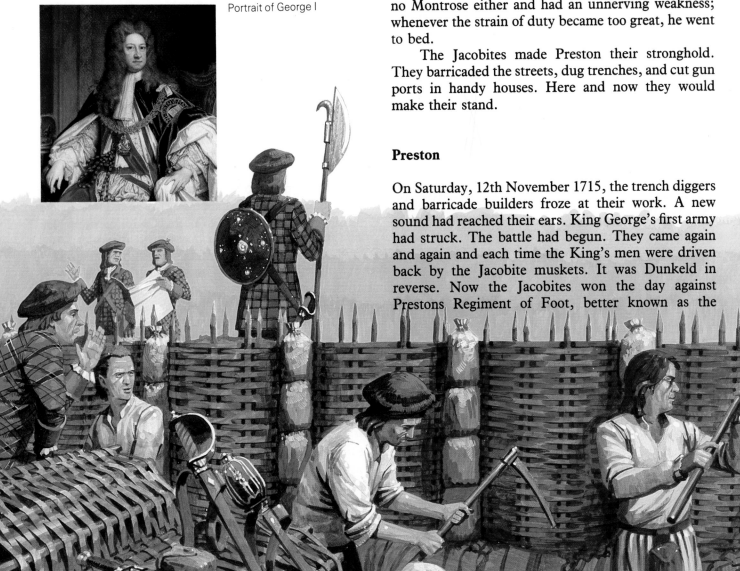

Portrait of George I

Crossing the Forth

Down through Fife, Old Borlum led his men and in the autumn darkness silently crossed the twenty miles of black Forth to North Berwick. It took two nights and a fleet of fifty small boats rowing backwards and forwards to transport his two thousand men, and all of this he kept hidden from watchful government eyes. Argyll had been outflanked and Borlum swung west towards Edinburgh, striking panic in the city. The Lord Provost sent express pleas to Argyll for help, but the Jacobites swept past the capital and down to Leith, rescuing their own men from the local Tolbooth jail and raiding the Customs House for brandy and provisions.

From Leith they turned south to be joined by the border Jacobites and some Englishmen. The force then crossed into England, and was threatened by approaching government armies at Preston. By now at least five hundred of the Highlanders had grown weary so far from their glens and had returned north. And Borlum's army was now under the command of Thomas Forster, M.P. for Northumberland. He was no Montrose either and had an unnerving weakness; whenever the strain of duty became too great, he went to bed.

The Jacobites made Preston their stronghold. They barricaded the streets, dug trenches, and cut gun ports in handy houses. Here and now they would make their stand.

Preston

On Saturday, 12th November 1715, the trench diggers and barricade builders froze at their work. A new sound had reached their ears. King George's first army had struck. The battle had begun. They came again and again and each time the King's men were driven back by the Jacobite muskets. It was Dunkeld in reverse. Now the Jacobites won the day against Prestons Regiment of Foot, better known as the

Cameronians. This time it was the Jacobites who held the city. This time it was the Cameronians who failed to take it.

On the following day, a second government army arrived to join the siege. Preston was surrounded. For the Jacobites there was no escape, only surrender. Their aimless drift south into England finished in disaster. Argyll though outflanked had suffered no attack and still held his ground at Stirling barring the Jacobite way.

Sheriffmuir

Before dawn on that same November Sunday, another Jacobite army came to its battle positions in the chill darkness of approaching winter. This was a mighty force, far greater than the Duke of Argyll's and it was drawn up on the low western slopes of the Ochil Hills by Dunblane. Now, in Sheriffmuir where Allan Water curls south in a tight bend, Bobbing John, Earl of Mar, challenged Argyll for the Lowlands of Scotland.

Though only two miles divided the armies, it took some hours for Mar to make out where the real strength of the government force lay. At last the clans were unleashed on Argyll and his Campbells. There were old scores to settle. Throwing off their plaids in the frosty air, the Highlanders hurled themselves forward in a screaming slashing charge and drove back the Duke's right wing in hopeless flight. At the same time Argyll's cavalry surged against Mar's right wing and thrust it back in wild confusion. In a swirling fury of shrieking pipes and yelling men, of clashing steel and spattering muskets, the battle lines swung crazily round like some great wheel of tartan and redcoat, throwing one half to the north and the other to the south. Both sides rose to glorious victory. Both sides tasted bitter defeat. And the Jacobite ballad maker sang:

There's some say that we wan,
Some say they wan,
And some saine that nane wan at a', man
But one thing I'm sure,
That at Sheriffmuir,
A battle there was that I saw, man
And we ran and they ran
And they ran and we ran
And we ran and they ran awa', man.

The Jacobites had failed to break through to the Lowlands. Their rebellion of 1715 was lost. Those who had fought to place James Stuart, the Old Pretender, on the throne had failed and though he did arrive in Scotland, at Peterhead just before Christmas that year, his cause was already doomed.

Those who had fought against the hated Union failed too. Once again it had survived. Only the Highlanders, with hearts set on revenge and plunder won any kind of victory on the Jacobite side. The land was again at peace and the clansmen returned to their mountain glens.

Years of Peace

The government of King George I meant to keep this peace and took milder than usual action against the rebels only because too many Scots were at least partly on the Jacobite side, not wanting James as King, but hating the Union and England. Harsher punishment might have brought more rebellion.

In fact rebellion did come again four years later in 1719 but it was a feeble affair. The Spanish had promised five thousand troops, and weapons for thirty thousand more, for landings in England and a smaller force for Scotland. Bad weather scattered the fleet and in the end only three hundred soldiers made the crossing. They were joined by some wary clansmen, men from Athol, Camerons and Mackenzies and the MacGregors of Rob Roy. The Highlanders stayed only for a day's fight in narrow Glenshiel. At nightfall they returned quietly to their mountain homes and left the Spaniards to surrender to the Government army.

General Wade

General Wade was sent north to keep order in the Highlands. He was to finish what Gnaeus Julius Agricola, Roman Governor of Britain, had begun seventeen centuries before. Again the men of the north paved the roads that would carry government troops swiftly through troubled country; again they laboured at bridges to shorten the military routes. For ten years the work went on. Forty stone bridges were built and hundreds of miles of good road were driven deep into the heart of the brooding clan lands. The remote glens were opened up and strongholds at Fort William, Fort Augustus and Fort George linked. The Highlanders watched and waited, hating the roads but raising no hand against them.

General Wade's bridge at Aberfeldy

The Black Watch

Companies were formed from the clans loyal to King George to help keep the Highland peace. They wore a government tartan of dark green and became the famous regiment of the Black Watch. Other clans were disarmed. At least, what arms could be found were taken from them, usually rusty weapons and faulty or cheap imported muskets. The good ones lay hidden for another day. And for all George Wade's efforts to quieten the north, that day came. When it did it was a new generation of clansmen that rose to the call, a generation that remembered nothing of the 'Fifteen and nothing of Stuart kings. Even the Union was almost forty years old.

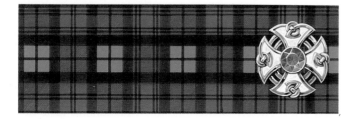

Charles Edward Stuart

On the 23rd July 1745, a French frigate put safely into harbour on the tiny Isle of Eriskay in South Uist. The small party of seven and their leader, a young man plainly dressed in a blue coat, were met by a local Clan Chief who advised them to go no further, to go back. The young leader replied stiffly 'I am come, sir, and I will entertain no notion at all of returning to that place whence I came . . .' The following night the frigate and its company slipped secretly from the harbour, unseen by the government man-of-war that had shadowed them on their stormy northern voyage. Via the Isles of Coll and Rhum and Eigg the vessel approached the mainland. At dawn it was skirting the Point of Sleat on Skye's southern tip and by mid-day on July 25th it tied up at Loch-nan-Uamh, between Arisaig and Moidart. For the band of travellers, the welcome was no warmer here on the mainland than it had been on Eriskay. It seemed they had come a long and stormy way to little purpose.

Local chiefs came on board again to advise the party to leave. But the personality of the young man in the plain coat touched the hearts of the clansmen and his urgent pleas were heard. The MacDonalds of Keppoch offered their support. It was enough. The party landed at Moidart and sent the frigate back to France. With only seven companions and a promise of help, Charles Edward Stuart, better remembered as 'Bonnie Prince Charlie', had come home to claim the throne for his father James, and to raise the Jacobites once more.

The 'Forty-Five

On the 19th August 1745, on the green braes of Glenfinnan, the lonely figure of Prince Charles watched the horizon, hope sinking, for two empty hours. At last the Camerons came into view, marching in two lines, about seven hundred of them, and with few weapons. But it was a beginning. The Young Pretender now had an army. That day the Marquis of Tullibardine, one of the original seven companions, broke out the blue, white and red silk of the Royal Stuart's Standard. The 'Forty-Five had begun.

At once the King George II's Government was alarmed. A price of £30,000 was put on the Prince's head. Sir John Cope was ordered against the Jacobites. He should have held the Highland line at Stirling as the Duke of Argyll had done thirty years before. Instead he marched north to meet the advancing rebels. At the last minute, Cope lost his nerve and sheltered his army at Inverness, letting the rebels sweep south to Perth, which they took on 4th September. Panic gripped the lowlands.

A Race for Edinburgh

Sir John Cope sent urgent orders for ship transports to meet his army at Aberdeen and set out on a forced march there, from Inverness. The race to the capital was on, the King's men by sea and the Jacobites overland.

Prince Charles led two thousand from Perth on Wednesday, 11th September and swung south-west. He crossed the River Forth that Friday at the Ford of Frew barely nine miles upstream from Stirling. They struck east then to Linlithgow, which was taken that same week-end. Now the Prince's men were only sixteen miles from Edinburgh. Frantic city elders called out the volunteer guard to man the crumbling walls.

Down Scotland's eastern coast, from Aberdeen, Cope's fully laden transports were making all possible speed, but off-shore winds would prevent entry to the Firth of Forth. Dunbar, thirty miles from Edinburgh, would be their closest landfall, and that not until 17th September. Already Bonnie Prince Charlie was outside the city walls and the volunteer guard had lost all taste for battle. News of Cope's coming fleet raised their spirits and they tried to delay the Prince's men by arguing over terms of the surrender of the capital. But Jacobite patience grew short and the latest time-wasters were sent curtly back in the early hours of Tuesday, 17th September. Their coach clattered along Edinburgh High Street to the Netherbow Port which opened to receive it. The coach entered the Cannongate with an unexpected and unwelcome escort of eight hundred Highlanders led by Cameron of Lochiel. It was five o'clock in the morning and the capital had fallen to the Jacobites with hardly an angry word spoken. While Cope's government army scrambled ashore at Dunbar, heralds in Edinburgh were proclaiming the Prince's father, James Stuart, once more King James VIII of Scotland and III of England. Bonnie Prince Charlie had won the race.

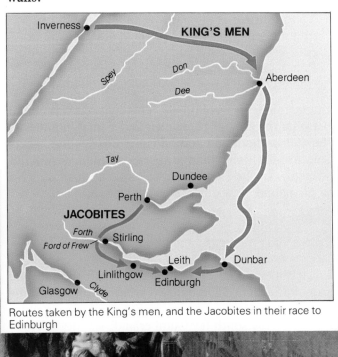

Routes taken by the King's men, and the Jacobites in their race to Edinburgh

Prince Charles entering Edinburgh

Prestonpans

But Jacobite rejoicing was short lived. A determined John Cope was now approaching from Dunbar with a well armed force, the only government army in Scotland. He meant to put down the Highland rebels. The Jacobites, now two and a half thousand strong moved east out of Edinburgh on 20th September and the two forces closed at Prestonpans. By the clever tactics of Lord George Murray, who had been with the Prince's men since Perth, the Jacobites surprised the better equipped army of King George II. The Edinburgh citizens, though they had admired the young prince, had laughed secretly at his shabby half-clad, ill-armed force. Sir John Cope had laughed too, calling them a 'parcel of rabble'. But the laughing stopped when the wild fury of the Highland charge was unleashed. Better equipped and better trained those government soldiers may have been, but they turned tail and fled before the tremendous din and speed of the attack. For the second time in a month the Jacobites swept aside Cope's government army of English and Scottish Lowlanders. Charles held the north. In London fears grew.

Wasting time

But Charles and his men did not at once thrust south to London. Instead, they wasted five weeks in Edin-

The Battle of Prestonpans

burgh celebrating the Prince's victory and attracting too few recruits. The British Government spent the same time gathering strength. Battle seasoned troops and German mercenaries were recalled from abroad to stiffen the courage of the government forces. When at last the Jacobites did cross the River Esk into England and pushed south by Carlisle, Preston and Manchester, there were two armies ready to meet them. George Wade commanded one at Newcastle and the other was under the Duke of Cumberland, King George II's third son, and cousin to the Prince. Now, in London, the recently composed National Anthem was nightly sung, with nervous enthusiasm and a new urgent prayer in its added fourth verse:

> God grant that Marshal Wade
> May by thy mighty aid
> Victory bring
> May he sedition hush
> And like a torrent rush
> Rebellious Scots to crush
> God Save the King

But not all Scots were rebels. This civil war was fought between the British plainsmen and a small number of the Celtic mountain folk. Prince Charles was never able to raise more than a quarter of the clan warrior strength. In the Lowlands there was no rush of Scots to his banner and much dour resistance.

Prince Charles turns back

In early December by trick and by bluff the Jacobite army had reached Derby, two hundred miles into the heart of England, unharmed. But twenty-four miles further to the south lay Cumberland; seventy miles to the north, was Wade. Each government army was bigger than the total Jacobite force. Worse still, news now came of a third equally strong force assembling for the defence of London. The Prince, with no hope of finding new recruits in England to swell his little army, had now no choice but to return north. It was a dismal prospect, the homeward retreat, but it was not a defeated army in flight that he commanded. Though Charles himself was deeply saddened by his failure to take London, his withdrawal was orderly.

Skirmishes

Twice the pursuers came too close and the Jacobites turned on them. On the 17th December, at Clifton, close to Preston, Cumberland's men came within a mile. There Lord George Murray sent a howling surge of Highland fury against the Duke's dragoons. They fled. Again at Falkirk the hounds came too close to their prey. This time Cumberland's troops were led by the brutal loud-mouthed Henry Hawley. He despised the Highland rebels and believed them unable to stand against well drilled cavalry.

Hawley, was so confident that he sent forward his mounted troops without infantry support against the advancing Highland front outside the government camp at Falkirk. Lord George Murray brought his line forward step by step to meet the thundering charge of the royal dragoons. Sword in hand and shield held high, he kept the line steady and tight as the tide of cavalry surged towards it. At ten minutes to four on the sleet-swept afternoon of 17th January 1746, and at a distance of twelve paces Lord George swung down his sword and the crackle of musket fire rippled along the Jacobite line from the MacDonalds of Keppoch on the right to Lord Lovat's Frasers on the left. The thundering onrush was broken. The King's cavalry fled the field. The wild clan charge that followed sent the remainder of Henry Hawley's army fleeing eastwards. By ten minutes past four, Hawley was defeated. The battle-seasoned troops recalled by the government had shown no more will to stand and fight than Sir John Cope's raw recruits. King George seemed no nearer an end to his troubles.

Typical Scottish swords and shield of the period

Retreat

But the Highlanders were tired of war for or against kings they knew or cared little about. They were Celts and they fought not for glory or conquest, nor thrones or empires, but to settle old scores, and to win plunder. The Jacobite army was simply melting away. Though they had smashed the best armies the Lowlanders could raise, they now retreated behind the Highland line.

By April 1746, fewer than five thousand weary half-starved men filled the ranks of the Prince. On Wednesday 16th of that month, by the chill grey of an overcast dawn, they limped into battle array on bleak Culloden Moor, a mile or two east of Inverness. Crouching there against the driving sleet they prepared to defend themselves against a fresh army twice their size and fully equipped. The fat young Duke of Cumberland himself would lead the government force. It included three battalions of Lowland Scots. It would be the final battle between the British Lowlands and the tribes of Northern Highlands, the last battle ever to be fought on British soil.

Of course the Jacobites should not have stood and fought in their weakened state and certainly not in that place. It offered nothing, no slopes to plunge down in those mightly clan charges, no cover from raking gunfire, no pits or marsh to slow the enemy horse. Lord George knew all this and at once described the moor as 'more improper ground for Highlanders' than any they had ever fought on. He wanted to refuse battle, and lead the government troops on a hopeless hunt through the misty glens as Bruce had done, and as Montrose had done. When Charles overruled this plan, Lord George saw but one slender chance.

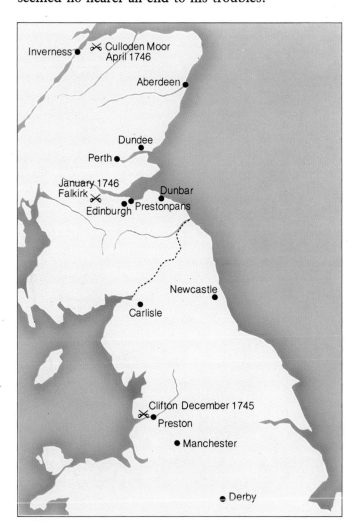

A Night Attack

Though his men were exhausted from bad nights under open skies and weak from gnawing hunger, Murray rallied them for a night raid on the Duke's camp at Nairn. Surprise was now their only hope. They must strike under cover of dark. But it took time to bring the men to their positions and time to push the weary columns from Culloden to Nairn, time they did not have. With four miles still to go Lord George saw their hopes fade in the brightening of the eastern sky. They could not now approach unseen. He had gambled and lost. The weary columns wheeled and started their grim trudge back to desolate Culloden, barely ahead of Cumberland's army. Men who had gone days without food, nights without sleep were now dragged from their promised rest by the thunder clap of the drummers' beating to arms.

The Battle of Culloden

For two sullen hours the armies faced each other across a half a mile of wintry moorland. And then it began. In answer to a Jacobite shot, came the deafening rumble of the Duke's guns, belching out their smoke and fire, in thirty long and deadly minutes of crushing cannonade. With their ranks terribly broken, the Highlanders were at last allowed to charge. Through the driving sleet and the raking musketry they pushed forward with what spirit they could raise and when they reached the steady line of redcoats, slashed wildly at the jabbing bayonets. In places they even broke through. But their charge had been held, turned, and was soon a frantic rout. Over a battlefield strewn with dead and dying, the Jacobites fled in hopeless disorder. The Lowland victors marched on in triumph, driving their bayonets into the wounded where they lay. More than a thousand, perhaps even two thousand of the Prince's men died on that grim and blood soaked moor. And Bonnie Prince Charlie himself was led from the field dazed and in tears, his cause utterly and finally lost.

Portraits of Bonnie Prince Charlie (**left**) and the Duke of Cumberland

Culloden

Cumberland's revenge

But, though the fighting had stopped, the killing went on. The British Government in London had decided that this time the rebellious Highlands would be crushed. The Scottish Lowlanders were just as determined. Prisoners and wounded would not be spared, though at Prestonpans and Falkirk the Jacobites, in victory, had treated enemy wounded as their own and their prisoners with mercy. Now the Duke, King George's son, would richly earn the shameful title of Butcher Cumberland, by which he is still remembered.

For five frightened months the Prince was moved secretly from place to place about the countryside as thousands of brutal soldiers, Scottish and English alike, scoured the land. Highland families were driven from their homes and their menfolk savagely beaten, even hanged, for what they would not tell or did not know. Yet, neither fear of the Butcher's men nor promises of untold wealth could prise Bonnie Prince Charlie from their safe-keeping as he was passed in desperate secrecy from clan to clan. When, in July that year, the baffled soldiers of the government stumbled too close, Flora MacDonald of South Uist took her Irish maidservant Betty Burke and sped in her boat across the Minch from Benbecula to Portree, on the east coast of Skye. Flora was arrested and imprisoned when it was later discovered that 'Betty Burke' was the Prince in disguise.

A prison ship interior

Prince Charles's Escape

From Portree, Charles crossed to Loch-nan-Uahm, to the silver sands of Arisaig where he had first landed a year before with an army of seven and hopes high. For two months he hid there in the caves and heather until at last he was daringly rescued, on 19th September, by a French frigate. He was carried back to France and to a saddened life of wanderings from country to country. 'Charlie's Year', as the Highlanders called it, was over.

But in Scotland the royal Butcher was still in business. By the end of 1746, one hundred and twenty people had been executed and ten times as many sold to plantations or banished. Seven hundred men and women had died in the disgusting filth of prison ships and jails. Countless nameless others perished at the brutal hands of soldiers who burned and slaughtered their way through the dark glens. As virtual dictator of Scotland, William Augustus, Duke of Cumberland earned a rise in salary of £25,000 and a place in the everlasting contempt of the nation.

Laws against the Highlanders

In London laws were made to quench the fiery spirit of the mountain people. On pain of death they were required to give up their weapons, even their bagpipes which were, to the southern government, instruments of war. On pain of transportation the wearing of the tartan was forbidden. Chiefs who were Jacobites had their lands seized, while, for all chiefs, their word was no longer the law of their clan. Only the King's peace would now be kept in the Highlands. The very clans themselves were being torn apart. And for five years or more after Charles had escaped to France the bitter hunt for hidden Jacobites went on. Yet, of all the harshness suffered by the Highlanders, none hurt more deeply than the stealing of their cattle. Thousands of beasts were driven from the glens for sale to the lowlanders while the hill folk could only watch and starve.

The Highland Regiments

And the men of the clans were lured away too, for service in His Majesty's armies, to win an Empire for the land that hated them. Britain's finest regiments, those that fought with the greatest honour and courage, with the least crime and desertion, were those of the Highlanders.

Worksection

The Last of the Royal Stuarts
Understand Your Work

The Union Under Stress
1 What happened to Scottish trade after the Union?
2 Why were Scottish manufacturers going out of business?
3 What did the £400,000 payment lead many people in England to think?
4 How did many Scots feel about the Union?
5 What sources of timber were preferred to those in the Highlands?
6 In what were Scottish soldiers now involved?
7 What did the Scots have little say in?

Jacobite Hopes
1 Who found new hope because of the general discontent with the Union?
2 Whom did they now support?
3 Who offered them help in their cause?
4 How did he try to help?
5 What went wrong?
6 What happened in 1713 which again threatened the Union?

King George I and the Fifteen
1 When did George I come to the throne?
2 Who was called Bobbing John?
3 Why did he change sides and join the Jacobites?
4 What did he do on his return to Scotland?
5 What unlikely allies gathered under the banner of the Royal Stuarts?
6 Why did they manage to forget their quarrels?
7 What support did Jacobites expect but not receive?
8 Who led the first strike by the Jacobite army?

Crossing the Forth and Preston
1 What route did Old Borlum follow?
2 How did he outflank the government army?
3 Did the Jacobites attack Edinburgh?
4 With whom did Borlum's force join on the march into England?
5 What made Thomas Forster MP a very poor choice of leader?
6 In what way was the fighting at Preston like the Battle of Dunkeld in reverse?
7 What finally caused the defeat of the Jacobites at Preston?
8 Who barred the way south to the main Jacobite army under the Earl of Mar?

Sheriffmuir and Peace
1 What else happened on the very day the Jacobites surrendered at Preston?
2 Who had the more powerful force at Sheriffmuir?
3 What was the result of the battle?
4 How did this affect the Rebellion?

5 Why did George I's government treat the rebels less harshly than usual?
6 Who was sent north to keep order in the Highlands?
7 How did he set about doing this?
8 What regiment was formed from clans loyal to King George?
9 How did the rebel clans manage to give up their weapons but keep them at the same time?

Bonnie Prince Charlie and the '45
1 Where did Prince Charles land?
2 What advice did Charles receive at first?
3 For whom was Charles claiming the throne?
4 Where was the Royal Stuart standard raised?
5 How did George II's government react?
6 Who won the race to Edinburgh?
7 How did the Highlanders enter the city?
8 What did the heralds' proclaim in Edinburgh?

Prestonpans
1 Who was the general in charge of Charles' troops?
2 What did he think of the Jacobite army?
3 How did the Jacobites gain an advantage over his army?
4 What was the result of Charles' victory at Prestonpans?
5 How did the Jacobites fail to take advantage of their success?
6 How did the people in London feel?

Charles and the Long Retreat
1 How far south did the Jacobites reach?
2 Why did he turn north again?
3 What happened when government forces twice came too close to the retreating Jacobites?
4 How did Lord George Murray deal with the government cavalry charge at Falkirk?
5 How long did it take the Jacobites to defeat Hawley's troops at Falkirk?
6 What weakened Charles' army?
7 Where did the Jacobites finally face King George II's army?
8 Why was this a bad place for Highland troops to fight?
9 What plan did Lord George Murray suggest?

Culloden and Revenge
1 How did Murray make one last attempt to gain an advantage over King George's men at Culloden?
2 What condition was the Jacobite army in when the fighting began?
3 What broke up and weakened the Jacobite ranks?
4 How many Jacobites were slaughtered in the rout?
5 What happened to the wounded and prisoners at the Battle of Culloden?
6 How many people were killed, imprisoned or deported after the '45?
7 How was Cumberland rewarded for this brutal work? How was he regarded by the people of Scotland?
8 What laws and penalties were imposed on the Highlanders?

9 What action by the government most hurt the Highlanders?

10 How else where the clans weakened?

Use Your Imagination

1 What did the Scots fear might happen if the Union was ended, that made them put up with England as a partner?

2 What do you think is meant by the statement 'Bobbing John was no Montrose'?

3 In your opinion was Old Borlum right to pass by Edinburgh without taking it?

4 Where do you think the Earl of Mar went wrong in his conduct of the '15 Rebellion?

5 In what way did the Highlanders find some success or victory in the failure of the rebellion?

6 What do you think is meant by – 'General Wade was sent north to finish what Agricola had begun'?

7 Why was he anxious to build roads and bridges?

8 A reward of £30,000 for the Prince was a massive sum of money equivalent to millions in today's money. What do you think this means that King Goerge's government felt about the danger they were in? What does the fact that the Prince was never betrayed tell you?

9 Does the verse which was added to the National Anthem tell you anything about how some people in England felt about Scotland, even forty years after the Union?

10 What do you think were Prince Charles' worst mistakes in his conduct of the '45

11 The Lowland Scots and the English both called the Highlanders savages. Do you think the events of the '45 rebellion suggested this was true?

Further Work

1 Here are two descriptions which will help you to understand what it was like after the Battle of Culloden. The first is by a little boy of seven, Ranald Macdonald, and the second is by a soldier of Cumberland's army. They are both quoted in a book called '*Lyon in Mourning*' by Robert Forbes.

Escaping . . .

'My step-mother, the gentleman, my eldest sister and me went to Ranach through woods and over mountains, on foot. And we used to lie on the tops of mountains and the gentleman used to roll me in his plaid with himself, and sometimes we walked all night when we heard the soldiers were near us. Upon a hill we spied our chief's son and all Keppoch's family, but we had very little time to stay with them for we heard the soldiers were coming that way. Then we parted, and travelled all that night on foot, and the next day till seven o'clock in the evening. Then we took our night's rest under two steep hills, were we had four miles to go for wood to build a little house of sticks and sods, and we had as far to go for water as we had to go for wood.'

Treatment of Prisoners by Cumberland's Men

(This was written by a Jacobite prisoner who escaped while under sentence of death. He then pretended to be an English officer writing about his experience. His name was John Farquharson.)

'But oh Heavens! What a scene open to my eyes and nose all at once; the wounded all feltering in their gore and blood, some dead bodies covered quite over with urine and dirt, the living standing to the middle in it, their groans would have pirsed (pierced) a heart of stone but our corrupt hearts was not in the least touched . . .'

2 Lord George Murray wrote to Prince Charles after the defeat at Culloden explaining his views on why the day had been lost. Here is part of that letter. Study it in your groups and see if you can make a list of reasons given by him.

'It was surely wrong to set up the Royal Standard without having positive assurance from his most Christian Majesty that he would assist you with all his might. . . .'

'As for . . . the management of your Army, we were all fully convinced that Mr. O'Sullivan , . . committed gross Blunders on many occasions. He, whose business it was, did not so much as visit the ground where we were to draw up in line of Battle, and it was a fatal error yesterday to allow the enemy so fair a field for their horse and cannon, and those walls upon their left, which made it impossible for our right to brake them, and we were exposed both to their front and flank fire. Col. Carr can testify that I urged Mr. Sullivan to take the ground on the south side of the water of Ern, which was strong ground, and very favourable for Highlanders, and which Brigadier Stapleton and Col. Carr had visited the day before at my desire. In short never was more improper ground for Highlanders than that where we fought. . . .'

'The want of provisions was another misfortune which had the most fatal consequences. Mr. Hay, whom you trusted with the principle direction and superintendency of them things . . . has served yr. R.H. most egregious (outrageous) ill; when I told him of the consequences of provisions, he said it was order'd, the thing was done, it would be gott, etc. But your R.H. knows the strait we were in. Had this Gentleman done his duty . . . our ruine might have been probably prevented. The last three days (which were so critical) our army was starved, and this was a great cause of our night march proving abortive, when we possiblie might have surprised the enemy and defeat them at Nairn, but for want of provisions a third of our army scater'd and went to Inverness and other places, and those who did march went so slow that that precious time was lost. The next day, the fatal day, if we had got plenty of provisions, we might have not only cross'd the water of Ern, but by the strength of our position made it so dangerous for the Enemy to have attack us, that probably that means the rest of our Army would have had time to have join'd us, and we would have had it in our power to have attack them night or day when we pleased.'

Landscape

By that dismal spring in 1746 when the straggling remains of Prince Charles's Highland army were swept from bleak Culloden, the Union of Scotland with England was almost forty years old. North of the border it was still disliked and the people were angered by the Duke of Cumberland's harsh dictatorship, and by new laws that too often seemed to favour the south. It seemed as though Scotland had become an occupied country once again.

Yet England was neither against Scotland nor for her. To most people in the south, Scotland was just part of the island which, like any other part, would have to get on with the business of surviving in hot and hard competition with the rest. And the Scots were to prove good survivors. With no more English wars to waste their homeland and drain their strength, they could now turn all their energy to improvement. Through the gloom that had darkened the land for centuries, since Alexander III had died at Kinghorn, there dawned a new golden age; an age of the mind, of reason and invention, of art and industry. But it wouldn't happen overnight.

In 1746 more than a million people lived in this northern kingdom, half of them in the Highlands, and almost all of them by farming. It was still a poor place of scattered hamlets where life was scraped from scanty soil in the same ancient ways. In a few bustling burghs trade thrived and burgesses prospered in the same old dirt and din. In the countryside there was little enough to be seen that was different, yet it was there that the changes would first take place. By 1746 they had already begun.

An Agricultural Experiment

Just north of Pathhead in East Lothian at a farm called Muirhouse (Murrays) a new kind of ditch digging was going on, as early as 1720. The soil dug up was carefully heaped to form a low boundary-wall which enclosed the spread of narrow humped rigs on which grew the scanty crops. On top of the earth wall, hedges were planted of thorn, privet, and elder. The close growing hedge plants would protect and shelter the farm while honeysuckle and occasional trees were added for their beauty. All the enclosed land was rented by one tenant. For the first time, run-rig had given way to fields. Instead of tilling scattered strips of soil, the farmer had all his land together.

Muirhouse farm was on John Cockburn's estate at Ormiston and was held by Robert Wight, but not on the usual short uncertain lease. To encourage improvements, Cockburn had granted his tenant a thirty-eight year lease with more to follow if he or his family so wished. And the improvements came, under Cockburn's advice. Not just the ditch with its hedge, but new and better ways of tending land and crops: proper drainage for water-logged ground; lime to sweeten the acid soil; the planting of grasses and clover seed for better pasture and haymaking; the rotation of crops and the resting of fields, ploughed but unsown; the growing of turnip, potato and wheat, alongside the old crops of oats and barley.

The Muirhouse experiment

Ormiston

John Cockburn did more. He rebuilt the village of Ormiston with wide tree-lined streets. He offered good building plots on good terms to his tenants if they would put up houses to his standards, stone-walled and roofs slated. He wanted a healthier place to live and work. Even now Ormiston is a handsome and spacious village, well planned and resting pleasantly in the soft valley of the River Tyne. He set up industries too for his tenants: making linen from the flax they grew, beer and whisky from the barleycorn. And wide plantations of trees were laid down to shelter the farmlands from the raking winds that carried away the goodness of the top soil. The new woodlands replaced those that had vanished as man had sought a place to live, material to build and fuel for his fires.

Ormiston today

Portrait of John Cockburn

Monymusk

Further north at Monymusk, twenty or so miles from Aberdeen, another man had work to do. Sir Archibald Grant had received the old Priory lands as a wedding gift from his father. But the place was a wilderness of weeds and stones. The thin exhausted soil was heaped in crooked rigs which straggled down the treeless braes. Without drainage the lower slopes and valley floor were sour and marshy. The River Don flowed, mean and uncertain, between its broken banks. The people lived in low hovels of turf and thatch and grew scanty crops of barley and oats.

Like John Cockburn, Sir Archibald Grant was a Member of Parliament. He had seen new methods of farming in England on his many journeys to and from Westminster. Now he bent to his task in the north. By enclosing the fields and clearing the stones; draining, ploughing and liming, feeding the scanty soil and planting the new crops, Sir Archibald transformed the miserable wastelands of bleak and treeless Monymusk into a rich fruitful valley. It took him forty tireless years of determined striving. Perhaps as many as fifty million trees were planted during this time and the estate was landscaped with riverside walks and sheltered gardens. By the now clear flowing Don this stretch of new and pleasant woodland was christened Paradise, for its peaceful beauty, a title richly deserved.

And Grant's tenants too lived a better life in better houses. They had a new stone church in which to pray and sing their psalms. When the great John Wesley preached there in the quiet of a summer evening in 1761 he said that the choir had sung the anthem after his sermon 'with such voices as well as judgment that I doubt whether they could have been excelled in any Cathedral in England.' That year and again three years later Wesley saw and remarked on the improvements Sir Archibald had made. Land that had been dreary moors was now aglow with ripe corn and the ground was as well tilled as most in the south.

Monymusk church

Improving the land

But even before these men had begun their work, even before the Union had taken place, Lady Huntly, herself from England, had brought English ploughmen with English ploughs to improve the estates of Gordon in Moray. In 1706 she began clearing and draining the heavy soil, and raising grass to make hay for winter feed. She also planted wide stretches of woodland and laid out new and lovely gardens.

The Honourable Society

From the Solway in the south to Moray in the north, Scotland was alive with the new farming. The business of improving agriculture excited England and the rest of Europe, but it gripped Scotland like a fever. In the summer of 1723, a meeting was attended in Edinburgh by important men inspired by the new thinking: dukes, peers and knights, Lords of the Court of Session and professors of universities; lawyers and judges, lairds and landlords, all dedicated to improving the quality of Scotland's farms. They formed the three hundred strong 'Honourable Society of Improvers in the Knowledge of Agriculture in Scotland.' From that first meeting until the fateful year of 1745 when the Society, along with many other things in Scotland, ended, they spread information, offered help and advice, and solved problems nation-wide with untiring energy. The poet Allan Ramsay wrote of them:

> Continue, best of clubs, long to improve
> Your native plains and gain your nation's love.
> Rouse every lazy laird of each wide field
> That unmanured not half their product yield.
> Show them the proper season, soils, and art,
> How they may plenty to their lands impart,
> Triple their rents, increase the farmer's store,
> Without the purchase of one acre more.

Books

And the enthusiasm reached people everywhere. In prison in Edinburgh Castle was a Jacobite rebel named William Mackintosh of Borlum. He was the same Old Borlum who had slipped two thousand men across the Firth under the noses of the Government forces. Now he had turned his mind to more peaceful things. In 1729 he published a book addressed to the most noble 'Lords and Honourable Gentlemen of the Scottish Nation in the British Parliament by a Lover of His Country'. He called it *An Essay on Ways and Means for Inclosing, Fallowing, Planting etc*. In it he attacked short leases and bad conditions for tenants and encouraged the enclosing of fields by hedge or stone dyke; the planting of trees, turnips, and grass for hay. He even suggested that a college of agriculture should be set up. Three years later he published another essay providing further ideas for better farming. And all over the kingdom the Scots lords and lairds were fascinated by the theory of agriculture. Booklets and essays poured out to be eagerly read and discussed in societies and clubs, to be consulted even by some tenant farmers. Yet for all the joy this wild enthusiasm brought to such men they were still few in number and there were many who were not nearly so happy.

Families were being evicted as their small farms were swept together to be enclosed for herds of cattle. The country folk who had used common pasture for grazing their own animals were now barred by hedge and dyke. As usual, many were suspicious of new ideas simply because they were new. Grant of Monymusk and Cockburn of Ormiston fought a long struggle against the last group, the tenants who refused to do as they were told. Long and secure leases were offered only on condition that the new ideas were put into practice. But this did not always work. In an angry message to his people in Monymusk, Sir Archibald complained that 'Your misfortune is not the want of good soil but your mismanagement of it ... you don't plant what you are bound to do, nor preserve and train them when planted... For God's sake, then, be roused by the example of others and by your own reason to pursue your true interest...'

Victims of the enclosure movement are evicted from their home

AN
ESSAY
John ON *Hume*
WAYS and MEANS
FOR
INCLOSING, FALLOWING,
PLANTING, &c.
SCOTLAND;
And that in Sixteen Years at fartheft.

By a LOVER of his COUNTRY.

EDINBURGH,
Printed, and Sold at Mr. FREEBAIRN's Shop in
the *Parliament Clofs*; and at Mr. MILLAR's, over-
againft St. *Clement's* Church in the *Strand, London*.
M. DCC. XXIX.

Title page of William
Mackintosh's *Essay*

'Levellers' wrecking dykes

A Response to New Methods

But people who had lost farms and pasture could not pursue their true interest. They had lost their living. Some who could afford it, emigrated to America and of the others some fought back. They formed into bands and rode through the southern counties of Scotland tearing down the hated walls. They were called the 'Levellers' and though the army was called out against them and those who were caught transported to distant exile, the struggle went on for twenty years. Of them and their fight a ballad maker sang:

Against the poor the lairds prevail
With all their wicked works,
Who will enclose both hill and dale,
And turn corn-fields to parks.
The lords and lairds they drive us out
From mailings where we dwell;
The poor man cries, 'Where shall we go?'
The rich says, 'Go to hell!'

Portrait of Lord Kames

With so many people ready to hold out against the new ways for reasons both good and bad, progress at first was slow. Not until 1760 did the pace quicken. Then a sudden torrent of change came roaring through the farmlands of Scotland. In his south Perthshire estate of Blair Drummond, Lord Kames, High Court Judge and by now seventy years of age, embarked upon a mighty scheme. Under the wide Moss of Kincardine, Kames knew that there lay more than eighteen hundred acres of good earth suffocated by a thick blanket of peat three metres deep, ten million tons of it. Only when the peat was removed would shining cornlands and fresh pasture stand in place of the sour black bogs on the fertile Carse of Stirling.

Reclaiming the land

It was a daunting task but his lordship was a determined old gentlemen and he had a plan. The Moss of Kincardine was held in the fork of two rivers. On the south flowed the upper reaches of the Forth, on the north and higher on the braeside, its tributary, the River Teith. Lord Kames's greatest problem lay not in digging up the peat, but in the enormous labour of carrying away such vast quantities, particularly in a land without proper roads and with few enough wheeled carts! The two rivers held the answer. On the banks of the Teith he constructed a gigantic wooden wheel. The turning of this huge apparatus raised the level of the river water by more than five metres where it was held in reservoirs behind closed sluices. When the sluice gates were opened the downrush of water swept the cut peat along specially formed channels to float away on the River Forth as it snaked and twisted along the valley floor. In the years left to the elderly lord, more than a third of the great Moss was laid bare, adding six hundred acres of fine farmland to Blair Drummond. His son carried on the work.

The energetic old judge did not confine his efforts to reclaiming the great Moss. He did not stop even at the general work of enclosing and draining his fields, the tilling, liming and sowing, nor yet at the acres of tree planting. He was a road maker and bridge builder too. And he even found time to cast a sharp scientific eye on the claim by England's great expert Jethro Tull, that plants grew by eating particles of soil through their roots. Weighing soil in a pot before and after proved this idea to be quite wrong. He set down all his ideas in a book called *The Gentleman Farmer*, which was published in 1776, when he was eighty. In it he said of one Scottish farming tool that it was 'more fitted to raise laughter than the soil.' Lord Kames made no profit from his mighty labours; his reward was only in the joy of honest and successful striving. He died aged ninety.

Lord Kames' reclamation of the Moss of Kincardine

Improving the soil

The clearing of the peat was not the only major engineering work in progress. In Angus, John, Earl of Strathmore, was directing work on the banks of the Loch of Forfar. Wide deep ditches were being dug towards the loch. When they were completed and the final dams broken the water that rushed out along the ditches lowered the level of Loch Forfar by five metres. Now Strathmores men could dig out the rich layers of shell marl, which would serve the farmers needs instead of lime. The now brimming ditches were used as canals on which to transport the marl to where it was needed on the estate and beyond.

A threshing machine

But not all engineering was on this huge scale. Ingenious men were hard at work solving other problems. It was then common farming practice to separate chaff from corn by threshing it between two opposite doorways in the barn and letting windy Scotland's drafts blow away the light husks fron the heavier grain. But even in Scotland the wind did not always blow to suit the farmer so James Meikle invented a machine to winnow the grain whatever the weather's mood might be. Sadly many thought it to be a machine of the devil that tried to 'interfere with the laws of God'. It was only slowly accepted.

Meikle's threshing machine

A new plough

No such superstitions troubled the mind of James Small who was busy in his workshop at Blackadder Mount two miles south-west of Chirnside in Berwickshire. From the early days the fields of Scotland had been turned by the heavy clumsy wooden plough dragged through the clinging earth by great teams of sweating beasts and struggling men. James Small thought it time for something better. His new plough replaced the wooden coulter that butted its way through the soil with an iron knife blade to slice a vertical cut. Here was a plough that could be drawn by a pair of horses and handled by one man. Teams of four men and eight, even twelve oxen were soon to disappear.

The leading edge of the blunt share was now of sharpened iron to slice beneath the sod, to the right hand of the clean down-cut made by the iron coulter. And the soil cut free in this was not shoved aside by the straight rough face of wooden mouldboard, but smoothly raised up and turned over by the outswept curve of a carefully shaped iron mouldboard.

Stone and slate houses

Prosperity

By 1815 in all the counties of Lowland Scotland, progress was racing, and with it the minds and ways of the people were changing. The new farmers were no longer content with earthen hovels shared with the beasts of their fields. Now there were solid stone houses with roofs of slate for the tenant farmers. Fields were all enclosed with stone dykes or close grown hedges of thorn and privet and the long humped strips of the old run-rig were nowhere to be seen. The new wheatlands extended to more than a hundred and forty thousand acres. Fields of potato and turnip, cabbage and carrot covered wide areas of the countryside. Less than a quarter of Scotland's whole land mass would support crops but that quarter was now expertly farmed to produce rich harvests of new foods as well as the barley and oats of old.

In East Lothian and in the border country, in the coastal plain of Moray and the valley of the Mearns in Kincardine, the rich farmlands were given over to crops only. Elsewhere the farming was mixed, grain with grazing. On the moist green banks of the Clyde and in North Ayreshire dairy farming prospered and milk, butter, and cheese were produced to meet the demands of the growing city of Glasgow.

A rising standard of living

The common folk ate better and dressed better. No longer did children take a lump of pease bread to school for dinner. Now they could have wheaten bread and butter; sweet milk, eggs and cheese, even roast meat. And the young ploughman could stride out in fine style on Sunday in his blue coat of English cloth and smart velvet waist-coat, a shirt with ruffled front and cravat of snow bright linen. He would wear blue corduroy breeches with fine cotton stockings and calf skin shoes fastened with shining buckles. A black three cornered hat in felt or velvet covered his head and in his pocket he would carry a watch by which he might time the minister's long sermon.

Brass and silver Highland brooches

And the young ladies were bright in calico prints or silk gowns from England. Their bonnets too were silk, and gay with coloured ribbons. They wore scarlet plaids or hooded cloaks and capes.

A Statistical Account of Scotland

As the nineteenth century opened, the population, rapidly approached two million. It was healthier and fitter than it had ever been and the future brimmed with hope and confidence. Sir John Sinclair was one of the giants of the great farming revolution. He had once led more than a thousand men on a peacetime battle against the rugged Scottish landscape and driven a road across the marshy slopes of Ben Chielt in South Caithness, all in a single day. He it was who set himself the huge task of preparing a detailed account of the nation's state of progress in lifestyle, industry and farming in every parish in the kingdom, a decade's labour published in twenty-one large volumes – the first *Statistical Account of Scotland*. Sir John saw in all his facts and figures a dazzling future for the kingdom in the north.

In less than a century Scotland's farming soared from the depths of primitive misery to undreamed of heights in the expert production of food. The new high farming of Scotland attracted admirers not just from England but from two continents. The pupil had become the teacher.

Portrait of Sir John Sinclair

The Highlands

All this was true, only of the Lowlands. Further north and to the west there was another bleaker tale to tell. To cross the Highland line was to enter another world. There, where half the nation lived, clansmen still scratched what miserable living they could from the thin soil of their straggling braeside run-rigs. Shaken by the long vengeance of the British Government, there was little prosperity except on the fringes, and famine was still written on the weary faces of the hill folk.

But it was not Cumberland's soldiers who brought the worst distress. It was quite another lowland intruder – sheep. These timid invaders arrived in 1762 from the green valley of the River Annan and settled to graze the rougher pastures of Perth. And they thrived. With wooly coats to ward off the winter chill and fresh young heather shoots for food all the year round, the sheep found the Highlands much to their liking.

Sheep farming

The sheep, together with man's greed and the problem of too many people for the poor farmland to support, caused a terrible change in the Western Highlands of Scotland. Sheep needed wide clear pasture to graze and for this the sheepmen offered high rents. Wide clear pastures meant that the scattered crofts with their scanty run-rigs had to go.

Clearing the Highlands

And so began in the Highlands a bitter period that time has not yet sweetened. To be turned out of croft and home by grinding poverty and failing harvest was part of the harsh life in the north. But now men, women, old and young, and helpless children, whose forefathers had scraped out their living, generation upon generation, in the glens and straths of the mountain country, were brutally driven from their squat hovels by their own clan chiefs, the chiefs whose duty it was to protect them. To the Celts, the land was theirs and not the property of some overlord. They now learned a new and bitter lesson as, with little warning, they were cleared out of house and farm by sharply increased rents, and by fire and force if necessary. At one time they had been valued as the proud swordsmen of their warrior chiefs but that day had now gone and there was no longer a place for them in their own mountains.

In Sutherland alone more than fifteen thousand hill folk were evicted from their homes by the Duke and his henchman James Loch. They were sent to find what living they could on the narrow shelf of land by the sea or across it in the New World. During these long cruel years tens of thousands left their native highlands in tightly packed vessels owned by men as brutal as those who had burned the roof timbers of their crofts. The laws that required the sailing ships *Sarah* and *Dove* to carry fewer than five hundred slaves did not prevent them cramming in seven hundred wretched homeless passengers, as they put out from Fort William in 1801. Yet those who did survive the dreadful misery of the long crossings gave all their great gifts of mind and heart to the building of a new life in the towns and plains of Canada and America. But it was their second homeland and not by their own choice; a whole way of Scottish life had begun to fall into decay.

On Culloden Moor the hill tribes had been defeated and the lowland government afterwards destroyed the whole clan system. Then followed the years of the sheep and the burnings when human beings were cleared from their lands to make way for the new and more profitable 'four-footed clansman'. The greater wealth it brought was enjoyed by only the rich landowners. The hunter warriors of the mountain country in Scotland were to perish before the plainsmen, as would the Red Indian in America, and their hills would be inherited by the lowland farmer whose progress they had seemed to threaten.

Clearing the crofters

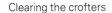

Townscape

For more than a century after the death of Queen Anne in 1714, the crown of Great Britain passed from one George to another – father to son, to grandson, to son – the First, Second, Third and Fourth. Throughout the Georgian years much more than farming prospered in the kingdom of Scotland, though none of it could have done so but for the improved methods of food production. A better fed nation, greater in numbers and strength, had wealth enough and time to face tasks and projects more ambitious than mere day to day survival.

Glasgow

In the west, on the north bank of the Clyde where it was wide and shallow, and where men for centuries had made their crossing place, the city of Glasgow grew. Until the Union it was a neat little city, clustered on either side of the half mile of High Street between the Cathedral at the north end, and the old University College with its pleasant meadowland reaching south towards the lazy flow of the river. There, in the shadow of the Merchant Hall's high and slender steeple, the river was spanned by the stone arches of the Old Bridge. Carts and horsemen crossed at a price, or forded the shallows free of toll, amongst men fishing, women at their laundry and the paddling children. Little lug-sailed skiffs and barges too plied the placid stream, carrying goods to and from larger vessels at their moorings in the deeper water by Dumbarton and Greenock.

An early view

About twelve thousand people lived in this small area between the Cathedral and the river. The better off had flats in the tenement buildings while the poor occupied low cottages. Neither were more than simple, badly lit, dwellings. From both, daily trips were made to bring fresh water from the city wells. But Glasgow was a neater and healthier place to live in than most cities, and visitors were impressed by it. Daniel Defoe, who was once an English spy in Scotland but is better remembered as the man who

wrote about Alexander Selkirk's adventures in the book called *Robinson Crusoe*, thought it 'the beautifullest little city in Britain'. Another traveller, Captain Bart, one of General Wade's engineers, reported that it was 'the prettiest and most uniform town that I ever saw; and I believe there is nothing like it in Britain.' He said that looking from the spacious Glasgow Cross he could view four handsome streets, (Trongate, Saltmarket, Gallowgate and High Street) with uniform houses of smoothly dressed cut stone with good windows.

Growth of trade

But the Union was to change this 'little city', that and men with a mind for business. Now that the Scots were free to trade with North America, men like Alexander Spiers of Elderslie and James Ritchie of Busby, John Glassford of Douglaston and William Cunninghame of Lainshaw in Ayrshire, seized the chance to set up new enterprises. They became importers and exporters, trading with the New World. They brought to the Clyde cargoes of tobacco-leaf and sugar for refining, rum and hardwoods, lemons and limes. And they sent out the kind of goods that new colonies required – coarse strong linen, iron tools for farming, carpentry, and building; pottery and glassware; furniture and leatherware.

Glasgow prospers through trade

The Tobacco Lords

So successful were these Glasgow men of business that by 1770 they were importing more than half the tobacco that came into all Britain, twenty million kilos of it. Almost all of that they exported to France. They made and lost huge fortunes and are remembered as the 'tobacco lords'. They were not men of rank from the 'right' families, but hard-headed traders whose wealth set Glasgow spreading westwards, naming its new streets after distant ports of call – Virginia Street, Jamaica Street, and there is a Glassford Street too. William Cunninghame's princely mansion still stands at the west end of Ingram Street. It was used as the Royal Exchange for more than a century and was the heart of Glasgow's trade and business. To-day it serves the community as a library.

Glasgow City Library, formerly the Royal Exchange

Glasgow flourished. Before the century was out it stretched west beyond Buchanan Street and south over the river. The population grew five-fold to more than sixty thousand, and in only another fifty years it would reach two hundred thousand. Now the rich had separate houses, even grand mansions, built around Blythswood Square, while the not so well off made do with flats above their businesses on the west side of Glasgow Cross. The poor lived where they could, huddled under what roofs they could find or in the converted flats left by wealthier tenants who fled before the sweeping advance of industry. These better houses were divided up into smaller units and soon decayed into the great warren-like slums of the Gorbals on the south bank.

Edinburgh

Over to the east Edinburgh too had begun to grow. But here the story would be a different one. In the first half of the century the population had doubled to reach fifty thousand. All were crammed tightly within the city's ancient walls. When no more space was to be found at street level they built on the roof tops – storey upon storey, their gable fronts like giant stone arrow-heads pointing skywards. Eight, ten, twelve, even thirteen storeys high the soaring flats towered over the wide 'royal mile' of cobbled way from the Castle perched on its rock, by Lawmarket, High Street and the Cannongate, past the Old Tolbooth, called by folk the 'Heart of Midlothian', and Parliament Hall; past the High Kirk of Edinburgh, called St Giles' Ca-thedral, and the Mercat Cross; and on down to the Palace of Holyrood. To the right and to the left gloomy wynds and vennels, shut off from sunlight, squeezed between the lofty blocks.

St. Giles' Cathedral,
Edinburgh

Inside the tenements, the folk were stacked by rank and riches, descending in wealth as they rose above the street. In the attic in single rooms, and also in the basement, lived the poorest tenants. On the ground floor, were the shops. Between these were the layers of the well-to-do, lawyers, merchants and doctors, even noblemen with spacious flats of six or more rooms. But all pushed their way up and down the same dark narrow stairways and all fetched water from the same city stand pipes. The capital city of Scotland was still the bustling burgh of old but now with more people and more noise, with more dirt and more smell.

A plan for the city

Not until nearer the end of the century did Edinburgh break out of the crumbling stone shell within which it had sheltered since the unhappy days of Flodden, and spread graceful new wings by its northern edge. It was the vision and bold energy of George Drummond, six times Lord Provost of the Capital, that set the great city stretching north over the green fields between Calton Hill and the Water of Leith, and on to the sea. The Provost's dreams were realised by the prize winning plans of a young architect called Craig. From six entries in the Town Council's competition of 1766, James Craig's was judged the best. To his pattern the farmlands north of Edinburgh would bear a noble harvest in shining new stone; public buildings and private houses in broad streets and spacious squares with fresh green lawns and formal gardens. The new town would be a vastly different place from the old with room to breathe and the sunlight overhead.

The plan itself was simple enough. There were to be three long streets, straight and wide and a grand square at each end. The principal way lay in the centre and was thirty five metres broad. It would be named George Street, after King George III. It was flanked on the north by Queen Street and on the south by Princes Street, both about thirty metres wide. All three were crossed five times in their mile length by wide side streets. Everywhere the names honoured Church and Monarch.

Making a start

The way to the new town site was opened in 1772 by the building of North Bridge. It was to link past with future. Now could begin the mighty work of laying down Craig's elegant and perfect streets on a tumbling landscape of hill and dale, river channel and loch bed. There the Georgian builders of Edinburgh, with few stonemasons and little enough experience, erected their magnificent new townscape, as utterly different in its grace and form, from the ancient huddle it overlooked as the new farms of Scotland were from the miserable run-rigs they had replaced. It was a masterpiece of town design. A quarter way through the new century five thousand wonderful new houses stood proudly in their perfect ranks and files where the northern fields had been. Provost Drummond's dream was built in solid stone. Now the north had its Athens.

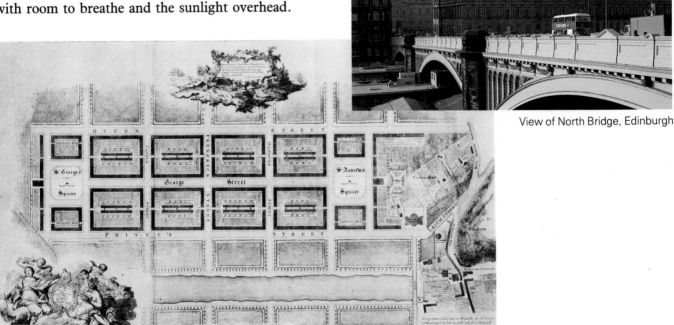

View of North Bridge, Edinburgh

Map of 'New town'

47

Class divisions

Not all of the Lord Provost's dreams came true. The gully between the old and new Edinburgh, spanned by the North Bridge, would remain as a class gulf between rich and poor. Out of the old royal mile and into Craig's new royal streets and squares came the people of wealth and rank, a trickle at first and then in flood. They set up their new high society away from the lesser folk amongst whom they had once thought it quite natural to live. The tall crowded tenements they left were now to be the homes of labourer and craftsman, shopkeeper and teacher, the poor and the diseased. The ancient huddle sank swiftly into disrepair, soon to be the slumland of Edinburgh.

In the narrow unlit lanes of the old town, stalked the prowling body-snatchers, Burke and Hare. They made a gruesome living providing corpses for medical research, plundered from fresh graves. Frantic people mounted cemetery guard and built iron cages over their newly dead to defy the grave robbers. Yet Burke and Hare were always ready to meet the demands of Dr Robert Knox who paid handsomely, asking no questions even about the freshness of the bodies that came to him from the shadows. Only when students attending Knox's demonstrations saw the bodies of people they knew personally to have been healthy just hours before, was it discovered how the grim pair came by their supply. They were now seeking the dead amongst the living, amongst those whom they thought would go unmourned. Burke was hanged on the evidence of the tall leering Hare, for which he was spared the gallows, only to be chased over the border by the enraged mob. Dr. Knox too, was driven from the city. Burke's wife escaped to Ireland. And the children chanted:

'Doun the close and up the stair,
But and ben wi Burke and Hare.
Burke's the butcher, Hare's the thief,
Knox the man who buys the beef.'

Such was never part of George Drummond's bold and sunlit vision of the new Edinburgh.

Iron caged grave in Greyfriars Churchyard

Dundee

On the Firth of Tay, the City of Dundee too had begun to grow. Here there would be no Georgian new town reaching out from the old, and no stately terraces of fine mansions. Instead those with wealth enough fled from the huge clatter of tenement dwellings huddled by the river and under the shadow of the massive linen and jute mills; from the awful problems of water supply and sanitation and the looming threat of cholera and smallpox. They moved east some miles to the quiet fishing place of Broughty Ferry where Charles Hunter had laid out a grid of parallel streets on the sloping links by the sea. Within the rapidly swelling burgh it was houses for workers to man the mills that were built.

Facies Ciuitatis ABERDONIÆ Veteris. The Prospect of Old ABERDIEN.

An engraving of Aberdeen in about 1820

Aberdeen

And further north beyond the Dee there were changes. Aberdeen, for centuries clustered around its castle, church and market, now began to expand. Never a walled city, it could spread outwards from the start, with no need for the soaring tenements of

Aberdeen today

Edinburgh's early growth. By the close of the century, in 1799, the northern port had begun its 'New Town'. As in the capital there was a loch to drain and hills to level before the plans of architects like John Smith and Archibald Simpson could be laid out on the tilting landscape of Deeside. Westward of the city grew a splendid grid, beginning and ending in noble squares, joined and flanked by streets, long and straight, broad and narrow all paved in sparkling granite and softened with lawns and gardens. In Georgian Aberdeen, unlike Edinburgh and Glasgow, the rows of fine houses and the grand public buildings, their smooth granite shining silver in the brightness of the sunlight, were mixed with darker humbler lanes and courts crammed with lesser dwellings for lesser folk. There was no gully to divide rich from poor in the 'Granite City'.

The move to towns

At the time of the Union, when the eighteenth century had just begun, nearly all of the million or so Scots were country folk. Their days were spent in scratching what meagre harvest they could from the mean and sour earth of their crooked straggling braeside run-rigs, and resting from their long toil in the huddled smokiness of low hovels of clay and thatch. No more than a fifth of their number were crowded in the cities and energetic little burghs finding a better prosperity in the buying and selling of goods or in the skilled labour of their hands. All over the land the least fortunate begged for their right to life, and famine was never distant. By the end of that century more than half the population, soon to reach two million, had become townsfolk and the high farming of the improvers gave food enough to spare. The people of the four cities alone, had grown from a total of sixty-four thousand to almost a quarter of a million and the cotton town of Paisley, only three thousand strong at the union, now took third place in the kingdom behind Glasgow and Edinburgh, housing thirty-two thousand. The kingdom in the north had become a land of towns and almost all of this since Culloden. And still the pace quickened.

The planners of the Georgian years had broken the ancient boundaries and let spread the cities of Scotland in splendid spacious new suburbs. They strode boldly, bending the unruly landscape to the regular geometry of their grand design. And they built in solid stone: Aberdeen in the hard silver of its sparkling granite, Edinburgh mellow in warm honey-stone, and Glasgow aglow in red sandstone. Brick they used almost always unseen for interior walls and this not simply because stone was always more plentiful, more convenient, but because it pleased the character of the Georgian Scots. English towns only a few miles over the border and no further from quarries settled for brick.

Worksection

Understand Your Work
Landscape

An Agricultural Experiment
1 What gave Scotland a chance to improve itself?
2 In 1746 how did most Scots make their living?
3 Where was the first farm that was improved?
4 What was done here?
5 On whose land were these improvements carried out?
6 Apart from improving the farm itself what else was done to encourage the farmer?
7 What improvements did this lead to?
8 What other steps did John Cockburn take to improve the living standards of his tenants.
9 What industries did he encourage?

Monymusk
1 What faults were there in the farmlands of Monymusk?
2 What sort of life did the tenants lead?
3 How did Sir Archibald Grant improve the farm output?
4 How long did this work take?
5 What did John Wesley think of Monymusk church when he preached there?
6 What did he think about the farmland?
7 Who had begun work in the north before Grant?
8 From where did the skilled farm hands come to improve the fields of the Gordon lands?

The Honourable Society
1 When was the Society formed?
2 What kind of people made up the Society?
3 How long did it last?
4 How did William Mackintosh of Borlum spend his time in prison?
5 What were some of the suggestions he made?

A Response to New Methods
1 What kind of people were not happy about the new ideas?
2 What did the evicted people do?
3 What happened to those who fought back?
4 When did the changes gather speed?
5 What did Lord Kames plan to do?
6 How much peat had to be removed?
7 How did he transport the peat away from his land?
8 What other work did Lord Kames undertake?
9 How did he show that Jethro Tull was wrong about how plants grew?
10 How was the shell marl obtained from Loch Forfar?
11 What was it used for?

New Tools and Prosperity
1 Why was the traditional way of separating chaff from corn unreliable?
2 Who invented a machine that did the job far more efficiently?
3 Why was it not popular to begin with?

4 How did James Small's plough differ from the old wooden type?
5 What sort of housing did the new farmers expect?
6 What crops were now being grown?
7 What kind of farming prospered in the Clyde Valley and in North Ayrshire?
8 Where did these farmers find a market?

A Rising Standard of Living
1 How had the diet of the people improved?
2 What was Scotland's population around the year 1800?
3 Was all Scotland enjoying the new, better life?
4 What was life in the Highlands like?
5 What were the causes of this?
6 Why were sheep suited to the Highland conditions?

Clearing the Highlands
1 Why did the run-rigs and crofts have to be cleared away?
2 What made the Highlanders so bitter about the clearances?
3 How many were evicted in Sutherland?
4 How was this done?
5 Where were they expected to go?
6 How were the evicted families treated?
7 What were the final steps by which the lowland half of the nation destroyed the half who lived in the mountains?

Townscape

Glasgow
1 What did Scotland's new prosperity depend on?
2 How was fresh water obtained for houses in the City of Glasgow?
3 How did Glasgow compare with other cities at this time?
4 What changed Glasgow?
5 What were the imports and exports that made Glasgow rich?
6 Where was the tobacco exported to?
7 What purpose does the mansion which was once William Cunninghame's serve today?
8 What was the population of Glasgow by 1850?

Edinburgh
1 How did Edinburgh house its growing population at first?
2 On what levels did the poorest people live?
3 When did Edinburgh begin to spread outwards?
4 Who was the driving force behind this scheme to enlarge the city?
5 Which architect won the competition to design the new town?
6 What was built to link the old and the new town?
7 How many houses were added by 1825?
8 What happened to the old town when the new one was constructed?

Dundee and Aberdeen

1 How was the expansion of Dundee different from Glasgow and Edinburgh?
2 Why did the wealthy move out of the city?
3 Who designed the new town at Broughty Ferry?
4 Why, unlike Edinburgh, was Aberdeen able to expand right from the start?
5 When was building begun there?
6 How did the layout of the houses differ from both Glasgow and Edinburgh?
7 What stone was widely used in the building of Glasgow?
8 Why did the Georgian Scots choose stone and not brick for their building material?

Use Your Imagination

1 What do you think were the advantages of gathering each farmer's ground together and protecting it with a wall?

2 Why do you suppose a long lease with more to follow might encourage a tenant-farmer to improve his land?

3 What do you think guided John Cockburn in his choice of industries for Ormiston?

4 What advantages would landowners find in encouraging their tenants to lead healthier lives?

5 Had Jethro Tull been correct about how plants grew, what would Lord Kames have found when he weighed the pot the second time?

6 In what way did the idea of good drainage alter the farmlands of Scotland?

7 How do you suppose ploughing was changed by James Small's new plough – time taken, animals used, manpower?

8 In what way did the improved food production of the farms help to cause the cities to grow?

9 In Scotland, over the centuries almost all the people had made their living by farming. How was this now changing?

10 In what way do you think the spreading of Edinburgh increased the gulf between the rich and the poor?

11 Do you think Dr. Knox knew how Burke and Hare kept up their supply of bodies?

Further Work

1 Read carefully the description on page 40 of how the chaff was separated from the corn by threshing. Discuss this in your group and make sure that you understand:
    a) How the grain is freed from the husk (chaff)
    b) How the chaff is removed altogether.
When this is done see if your group can do as James Meikle did and invent a machine for doing the job. Make drawings, notes – and a working model if you have time to show the workings of your group's invention.

2 Imagine yourself as a visitor staying at one of the new farms. You have always been used to the old type of lifestyle. Write a letter home describing all the wonders and comforts you have found.

3 The troubles with the levellers was caused partly by the *way* in which the new ideas were introduced. Can you think how the changes could have been introduced to avoid these upsets? How would you explain the new methods? What are the advantages? How would you keep hardship to a minimum? Prepare your 'new deal' so that it not only sounds better, but *is* better. Make up an advertisement which puts over your ideas in an attractive way.

4 Here is a translation of a Gaelic poem which shows how the Highlanders felt about the sheep and those who tended them. It is quoted in the '*Highland Clearances*' by J. Prebble:
'Destruction to the sheep from all corners of Europe
Scab, wasting, pining, tumours on the stomach on the stomach and hide!
Foxes and eagles for the lambs!
Nothing more to be seen of them but fleshless hides
And the grey shepherds leaving the country
Without laces in their shoes.

5 Here is a poem called '*Open Range*' by Kathryn and Byron Jackson:
> 'Prairie goes to the mountain,
> Mountain goes to the sky,
> The sky sweeps across to the distant hills
> And here in the middle
> Am I.
>
> Hills crowd down to the river
> River runs by the tree
> Tree throws its shadow on sunburnt grass,
> And here, in the shadow
> Is me.
>
> Shadows creep up the mountain,
> Mountain goes black on the sky
> The sky bursts out with a million stars
> And here, by the campfire
> Am I.

Every verse begins with three lines describing an open landscape and ends with two which are very similar. Study the poem carefully and then write your own poem about the old part of Edinburgh. You can call it '*Old Town*' and have as many verses as you like.

The New Scots

It was well on in the century, during the 1770's, before the well-to-do of Edinburgh deserted Cannongate and High Street for the lovely New Town, leaving their old tenement homes to sink into decay. They looked forward to a dazzling future north of the gully that to-day is Princes Street Gardens. Edinburgh had now entered its new golden age.

And yet it was there, in the heart of the old walled city, that Edinburgh's greatness was born. It was not only, not even mainly, for its new buildings that the capital deserved the title, 'Athens of the North'. Georgian Scotland was filled with men whose genius would light the way of progress. Edinburgh was to become the very centre of brightness in this dazzling new age of thought and learning. Suddenly it took its place beside, perhaps even ahead of, London and Paris in striving to enlighten the minds of men. It was a far cry from the breaking of their heads that had been the preoccupation of the northern kingdom for too many long years.

Allan Ramsay's wig and book shop

Allan Ramsay

In the old High Street by the Mercat Cross the poet Allan Ramsay set up his wigmaker's shop. But his real interest lay in stories and verse rather than hair-pieces and he traded more in books than wigs. Here he opened Britain's first lending library. His shop became a famed meeting place for writers and book lovers. His son grew up in a wonderland of books, but for all his joy in them, Allan Junior's great talent lay in painting. His gentle gracious portraits of people in splendid dress brought more and more of the high and the mighty to sit for him. In 1754 he formed a society to encourage art, science and industry and some of the greatest minds in the land became members; amongst them were David Hume and Adam Smith.

Allan Ramsay (**left**) and his son (**right**), both portraits by Allan Ramsay Junior

Edinburgh New Town from the Castle

Adam Smith

Adam Smith was a philosopher too. While Professor at Glasgow University he published the first volume of a series meant to offer a complete theory of society. It was called *An Inquiry into the Causes of the Wealth of Nations*. In it he explained how the making of wealth would 'enrich both the people and the sovereign'. And he showed the good and evil of new mass production methods. For example, ordinary household pins could be turned out at a rate of forty-eight thousand a day if ten men shared the eighteen steps of the process needed to make them, each man continuously doing his part of the manufacture. If one man did the whole job he would be hard put to produce a single pin in a day. But later in the book Smith warns that a man condemned to a life 'spent in performing a few simple operations . . . has no occasion to exert his understanding . . . and generally becomes as stupid and ignorant, as it is possible for a human creature to become.'

Adam Smith taught that the '*Wealth of Nations*' lay not in hoarded gold but in the fuel and raw materials of industry and in the labour of skilled men. And with an eye on the unfeeling practices that left so many poor in the land he declared that 'No society can surely be flourishing and happy, of which the far greater part of the members are poor and miserable.' It was only fair that those who created the nation's wealth by their own labour should have a proper share of it.

David Hume

Hume was amongst the first people to set up home in the New Town, in an elegant house by St Andrew's Square at the east end of George Street. He was a philosopher, seeking sense and order, purpose and direction in what seemed to be the aimless shifting and mixing of human experience and behaviour, the joy and the despair. His first and finest book was *A Treatise of Human Nature*. He believed there should be not only a science of the physical world but a 'science of man' too. Hume would be its 'Isaac Newton'. By experiment and close observation, the way people thought, felt and behaved would be better understood. Modern psychology is that science.

David Hume's fresh and daring mind startled society and not always pleasantly. What subjects he chose to study were often as disturbing as what he said about them. The title of his essay *A Natural History of Religion* shocked people who had never thought for a single moment that there could be anything 'natural' about the history of religion; people whose recent forefathers had willingly died at the stake for their particular shade of the Christian belief; people in whose life-time it had been thought proper to burn witches! That the essay should go on to suggest that religious beliefs grow out of feelings of hope and fear, and mainly fear, was outrageous. For such ideas the great philosopher was twice refused posts in the Universities of Glasgow and Edinburgh, though they did not prevent his warm friendship with many leading Churchmen. And his good humour prevailed. When his maidservant rushed in with the news that the fine new street in which he lived had been named St David Street and obviously thought it a case of mistaken identity, David Hume assured her that 'many a better man has been made a saint o' before!'

Title page of Smith's *Wealth of Nations*

AN
INQUIRY
INTO THE
Nature and Caufes
OF THE
WEALTH OF NATIONS.

By ADAM SMITH, LL. D. and F. R. S.
Formerly Profeffor of Moral Philofophy in the Univerfity of GLASGOW.

IN TWO VOLUMES.
VOL. I.

LONDON:
PRINTED FOR W. STRAHAN; AND T. CADELL, IN THE STRAND.
MDCCLXXVI.

Adam Smith

For his great book Smith was recognised the world over as father of a new science called Political Economy; it would change the way in which states handled their prosperity. And he had done so, not by applying the drab rules of the economics which people were later to use, but by extending his own philosophy of what was morally right to the business of managing the wealth of nations. Prime Minister Pitt saw his greatness and he and guests rose to their feet when the philosopher hurried in late to a meeting. Brushing aside Adam Smith's apologies, Pitt exclaimed, 'We will stand until you are seated, for we are all your scholars.'

David Hume and Adam Smith were the tallest of the giants who now lifted Scotland into the new 'Golden Age'. The twin cities of Glasgow and Edinburgh brimmed with new talent and their universities commanded international respect. Glasgow for its mathematics and philosophy, Edinburgh for its great medical school.

Joseph Black

It was to Glasgow University in 1756 that a young instrument maker from Greenock came to set up shop. Here he built and repaired scientific apparatus, and stayed to assist the great chemist, Professor Joseph Black, in his experiments on the nature of heat. Black was puzzled by the curious fact that no matter how much heat he applied to boiling water the thermometer rose no higher. Yet all that heat had to be going somewhere. In the end he proved that it was used up in converting water at boiling point to a gas at the very same temperature, a gas called steam. The disappearing heat he called 'Latent Heat', but it was the gas that particularly interested the young instrument maker. His name was James Watt. Later he would remember these experiments in his work on the steam engines which one day would bring a new power to the industry and transport of the world.

John and William Hunter

Scotland, too small to contain its own restless energy, overflowed, spilling its genius south across the border and beyond the seas. Men of science and men of art, men of peace and men of war offered their gifts in the service of other people in other lands. John Hunter and his brother William, barely able to read and write as children, became the foremost of surgeons, bringing science to the study of medicine and anatomy.

Portrait of David Hume

Prime Minister Pitt stands to welcome Adam Smith

John was the greater medical researcher and teacher. He insisted upon the importance of experiment. To his famous pupil Edward Jenner, discoverer of the vaccine which wiped out the killer disease smallpox, he instructed simply and repeatedly, 'Don't think. Try it!' And though both brothers performed their noble deeds of healing in London, it was to his old University of Glasgow that William left his valuable collection of medical specimens and his coins and medals, together with funds to set up the now famous Hunterian Museum.

Artifacts from the Hunterian Museum

The Architects

In architecture too it was the men from the north who set the pace. James Gibbs is remembered for his great London churches including St Martin-in-the-Fields and for the Radcliffe Camera, part of Oxford's great library; Colin Campbell for his graceful style which recalls the splendour of ancient Rome; Sir William Chambers designed Somerset House in London and the Royal Bank of Scotland building in Edinburgh's St Andrew's Square, with its marvellous dome pierced through by a galaxy of star windows which let in the cool daylight of the northern capital; the Adam brothers John, Robert, James and William, who changed the face of Britain.

The Adam brothers

Of the four Adams, Robert was the greatest. In his creative vision the ancient styles of Greece and Rome were joined with later ideas in elegant and delicate forms. Simple beauty was blended with ready purpose. Soon all Britain had the Adam-style, not only in the lovely exteriors of his great buildings but inside too, where Robert Adam designed everything including the furniture, right down to the shape and ornament of the tiny covers which swung over the keyholes in his beautiful doors. The whole country clamoured for it. From master builders to ornamental masons, from silversmiths to iron founders, furniture makers, book-binders, potters like the great Josiah Wedgwood, they all copied Adam. Everywhere, in stone and metal, wood and plaster, appeared his flowing garlands and delicate bows, his slender urns and gentle figures relieving plainness or lending graceful form to ornament and furnishing, interiors and exteriors. Those not wealthy enough to possess stately mansions by the great architect could at least warm themselves at his fireplaces. Even the humble could share the high tastes of the rich, with Wedgwood's 'Adam style' Jasperware proudly displayed on shelves and walls.

Most of Robert Adam's masterpieces were built south of the border, elegant country houses with sweeping stairways to pillared fronts and finely proportioned rooms. Some were even circular with hidden doors, and glorious plaster ceilings warmed by delicate picture panels set in pastel tints and gold lining. And always there were his wondrous fireplaces. For Glasgow he designed the great Royal Infirmary and in Ayrshire built Culzean Castle. In Edinburgh's New Town the lovely Register House and Charlotte Square, the University buildings too owe their grace and simple charm to the fertile mind of Robert Adam, foremost architect of his time.

The staircase at Culzean Castle designed by Robert Adam

Thomas Cochrane

In the City of Valparaiso on the western edge of distant Chile, there stands a splendid statue to the memory of a great national hero. His burial place is in London, in Westminster Abbey and when guards of honour stood duty there, they were soldiers of South America. On his tomb under the flags of Greece, Brazil, Chile and Peru are the words of Sir Lyon Playfair, Professor of Chemistry at Edinburgh University. They read:

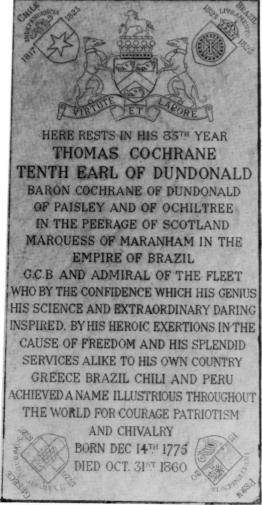

The tomb of Thomas Cochrane

Napoleon called him the Sea Wolf, but his name was Thomas Cochrane, 10th Earl of Dundonald, Admiral of the Fleet, and he was born in Culross on the north shore of the Firth of Forth.

In his tiny sloop, *Speedy*, whose total fire power in full broadside, unleashed no more shot than 'could comfortably be carried in Cochrane's pocket,' he held off the might of the French and the Spanish Navy, defying three battleships and capturing more than fifty of their vessels. Always outgunned and always outnumbered the Sea Wolf of Culross set the French coast

in turmoil with his dazzling seamanship and military brilliance, his iron nerve and inspired leadership.

In the early spring of 1801, the *Speedy* had not long left Port Mahon in Minorca when on the pale skyline of a mediterranean evening Cochrane sighted the billowing sails of a large frigate. A brief signal in Royal Navy code soon enough showed the warship to be hostile and it was now closing fast. *Speedy*'s only hope lay in flight. With all sail crowded on and the breeze freshening Cochrane made his run. Through that night and all the next day the *Speedy* strained before wind. Yet for all their dash the shadowing frigate drew steadily closer to the little sloop. As darkness fell again the chase was nearing an end. With just the glimmer of lights on Cochrane's ship to guide it through the night, the powerful warship plunged on and by the hour before dawn was upon its prey. In the cool grey light now lifting the eastern sky the warship's commander saw directly below his bows and where *Speedy* should have been, only a large wooden tub and a flickering candle lamp set within. Of Cochrane and his little ship there was no trace.

Barely six weeks later the *Speedy* found herself once more in the company of a powerful Spanish frigate. Cochrane had been in eager pursuit of two lighter vessels when suddenly out of the morning's thinning mists and dead ahead, loomed the tall menacing form of the thirty two-gun *Gamo*. It was a trap and escape impossible. Yet the Sea Wolf saw one slender hope – attack! On towards the mighty opponent, he urged his little sloop. Her desks cleared, her guns primed and her nerve rock steady the *Speedy* bore down on the surprised *Gamo*. Cochrane knew he must get close. As the distance narrowed a muffled boom and the whining hiss of a warning shot told all on the *Speedy* that they were now within range of the *Gamo's* deadly cannon and could be instantly sunk. Their own guns would not carry half that distance. Yet no one aboard the frigate could imagine that this tiny vessel really meant to attack a warship four times her size, gunned and manned more than six times as strongly.

As the *Speedy* drew past the long threat of the *Gamo's* gaping row of round black mouths, Cochrane broke out the American Flag at his masthead causing the Spanish gunners to hold their fire in doubt. Coming tightly about he brought the little sloop around the frigate's stern to pass her again, this time on the side away from the wind, this time under her true colours, the White Ensign of the Royal Navy. Now came the thunder. In rolling banks of red fire and black smoke the mighty broadside boomed forth. But the *Gamo* was pressed over towards the *Speedy* by the weight of wind in her sails and the aim was short. Great plumes of sea water fountained skywards drenching the sloop's decks but doing no damage.

56

As the men of the *Gamo* rushed to reload, the *Speedy* swung tightly once more and locked her masts with the lower yards of the tall frigate. Safely below the lowest angle of the mighty guns, the *Speedy* at last unleashed her own broadside, an upward hail of raking fire that tore through the planking and swept the main deck, towering above the British gunners. All attempts by the Spanish marines to board the little ship and quench the galling fire were thwarted by Cochrane who simply opened a sea gap between the vessels leaving the would-be boarders at the *Gamo's* rails, easy prey to the spattering musketry from below.

The *Speedy* and *Gamo* in action

To press home the advantage he seized so boldly, Cochrane was bolder still. He led his men on board the *Gamo*, fifty against three hundred, and by startling surprise, fierce courage and inspired bluff he drove the Spaniards into confusion and retreat. As the Spanish felt the fight turn against them Cochrane called loudly upon imaginary reinforcements. It was enough. At the very thought of hoards more fresher fiercer Royal Marines swarming out of their hiding place in the holds of the *Speedy*, to overwhelm the stricken *Gamo*, the Spaniards finally lost all taste for battle with this tiny white sailed dragon. When they saw their own flag coming slowly down from the masthead, they gave up the struggle and laid down their weapons. It was, of course, one of Cochrane's men who had lowered the Spanish colours in surrender! The little sloop with her crew at only half strength had taken captive the proud *Gamo*, sent to trap her. The tiny *Speedy* returned in triumph to Port Mahon leading by the nose her towering prize with almost three hundred prisoners held at their own cannon point by what few men could be spared from their proper duty of sailing the *Speedy*. But not for this amazing victory, not for any of the fifty or so other heroic clashes Cochrane had with the Spanish fleet during the first two years of the nineteenth century, did the great Admiral earn his title – 'Sea Wolf'. This respect was wrung from his new enemy Napoleon Buonaparte, Emperor of France and Conqueror of Europe. Through the summer of 1808 Cochrane prowled the curving coastline of southern France in his frigate, the *Imperieuse*. His lightning raids spread panic and disorder amongst the French defences forcing Napoleon to withdraw much needed front-line troops to defend his coasts.

In the late Autumn that year the Emperor ordered his men into Spain against rebels there who were resisting the power of France. When his column, more than six thousand strong and heavily armed, moved south through Catalonia it was the crew and the marines of Cochrane's frigate that barred their way at Fort Trinidad. For two weeks the tiny garrison held off the French army and inflicted serious losses before withdrawing under cover of naval gunfire to the *Imperieuse* anchored in the bay.

In the spring of the following year Cochrane produced yet another miracle of sea warfare when he shattered France's naval might in its safe anchorage at Basque Roads on the west coast of France, off Bordeaux. With explosive ships of his own invention he burst through the strong defences and sent the French scattering in panic. Only the unwillingness of the British fleet to follow the Sea Wolf's brave lead allowed some of Napoleon's fleet to escape.

Throughout the whole long war with France, Thomas Cochrane argued that the proper use of the navy could end the conflict swiftly, and that the whole French coast could be seized by naval attack and be in British army control in a matter of weeks rather than months. The nation would be spared the awful cost in blood and wealth of the snail-like land campaign led by the Duke of Wellington which ended in dearly bought glory, at Waterloo in 1815.

Yet for all his wondrous daring and seamanship Lord Thomas Cochrane could never properly overcome his enemies at home. So great a talent in a young man was as hard to accept as his lack of respect for empty authority. Even after the brilliant victory at Basque Roads it pleased the Admiralty to play down his part in it. It was left for a French prisoner who knew something of the matter, some time after to set the record straight. He declared that 'if Cochrane had been supported, he would have taken every one of our ships.' That Frenchman was Napoleon Buonaparte, sometime ruler of Europe.

In the House of Commons where he was ten years M.P. for Westminster, Cochrane made more enemies by loudly attacking their dishonest and unfair behaviour, and by exposing the deep corruption of the Admiralty itself. These were ten years of pain for the great sailor, when all who dared took their revenge and none more so than the Government itself. In early August 1818 Cochrane and his family slipped quietly out of port in a small fishing smack bound for Boulogne. Eventually he came to the distant waters of South America. There he would win greater glory and greater admiration than he had been allowed in his homeland.

Explosive ships in the Basque Roads off the west coast of France

As Vice Admiral of the Navy of Chile he attacked the great Spanish stronghold of Valdivia, five hundred or so miles south of Valparaiso, in February 1820. He had one warship, the fifty-gun *O'Higgins*, and because of a mishap it was now sinking. No one but this new Scottish Admiral would be mad enough to go on with the raid. To Cochrane the leaky boat meant simply they would have to hurry and the hopeless odds made it certain the Spanish would not be expecting them! With his usual mixture of magic and daring he threw the defenders into confusion. Under cover of darkness his landing craft dropped a few hundred marines and troops to create diversions and make attacks on strong points. Finally, when the battle hung in the balance the *O'Higgins* was sailed into full view. The sight of a warship crammed with reinforcements and bristling with heavy guns was quite enough for the Spanish. The sinking ship had, of course, no reinforcements but the defenders were not waiting to find that out. The mighty base had fallen to Cochrane.

His work·done in Chile he moved on to Brazil where as Admiral of the fleet he drove out the Portuguese, again outnumbered and outgunned.

After Six years brilliant service in South America, the now fifty year old Sea Wolf of Culross returned once more to his homeland, his great reputation greater still. When his frigate at last entered the narrow water at Spithead the Royal Navy thought it wise to honour his homecoming by firing a salute, though there were those in the Admiralty who might have been tempted to make more earnest use of their guns! But in Portsmouth when he disembarked the crowds had no doubt about their feelings, and they cheered and applauded him through the streets.

Sir Walter Scott

That October, back in Scotland, Cochrane and his wife Kitty attended the theatre in Edinburgh. During the performance mention was made of South America and at once that whole audience of his countrymen was on its feet to face the couple with long and loud applause, repeating again and again 'Cochrane! Cochrane!' Scotland's Sea Wolf was now her Sea King. And in the audience was a writer and poet who recalled Kitty's joy and pride in her husband that night. He wrote:

> Even now, as through the air the plaudits rung,
> I marked the smiles that in her features came;
> She caught the word that fell from every tongue,
> And her eye brightened at her Cochrane's name;
> And brighter yet became her bright eyes' blaze;
> It was his country, and she felt the praise.

But the poet is better remembered for his longer works, for *The Lay of the Last Minstrel*, *Marmian*, *The Lady of the Lake*; and for his stories too *Ivanhoe* and *Quentin Durward*; *Heart of Midlothian* and *Guy Mannering*; the three volumes of *Waverley* and more, more than twenty novels in all, and a history of Scotland called *Tales of a Grandfather*. He was Sir Walter Scott, one of the two giants among those writers who gave voice to the nation's creative energy in those Georgian years.

Portrait of Sir Walter Scott

'. . . her eye brightened at her Cochrane's name; . . .'

With his *Waverley*, Walter Scott began a whole new style of writing which fired the imagination of all Scotland, and beyond. There had simpy never been a story like it. Waverley teemed with breathless adventure set against high mountain glens and wild Scottish scenery, followed the bold deeds of Bonnie Prince Charlie's Jacobites and the King's men. And because the volumes were published without the author's name, all the nation was held in suspense, wondering who could have written them. For thirteen years he kept his secret though by then many had guessed that only he could have written such a story.

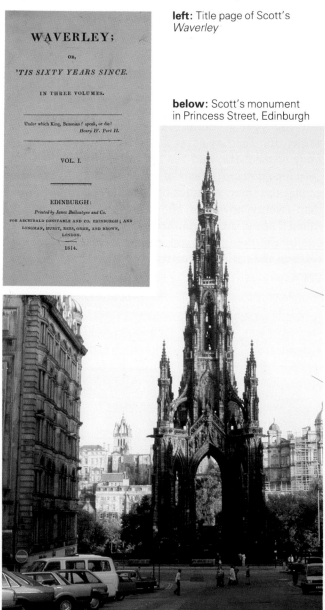

left: Title page of Scott's *Waverley*

below: Scott's monument in Princess Street, Edinburgh

Scott was no businessman. He made a fortune, lost it, and died in 1832, working to pay off his company's massive debts. But his monument in Edinburgh's Prince's Street bears witness to a talent that created a new and fashionable image for his native land.

Robert Burns

It was in the capital too, that a young man in his twenty-eighth year rode wearily into the Grassmarket in the late November chill of 1786. He had ridden on a borrowed horse from his home in Mauchline and carried with him the slim volume of his work called *Poems, Chiefly in the Scottish Dialect* and published by Wee Johnny Wilson, whose print shop was hard by Kilmarnock's market square. Already in Ayrshire the poems and songs in the book were eagerly read and recited by all who could lay hands upon it. Soon the Kilmarnock edition would bring wider fame to its writer Robert Burns.

In the rhythm of his fresh musical verse Burns had caught the living spirit of countryside and country folk, and he had done so in the language they used and understood. His poems spoke beautifully and vividly of things they knew and felt, of people they had met. Now all Edinburgh was at his feet, and in London too, the 'old and young, high and low, grave and gay, learned and ignorant, all were delighted, agitated, transported . . .'

Robert Burns riding into Grassmarket

Soon a new edition of his poems was needed and for this he chose William Creech. The Edinburgh edition would be produced in Creech's shop which stood beside Allan Ramsay's old wigmaking business. Like Ramsay, Creech turned his publishing house into a meeting place for the lovers of verse and story, books and ballads. Here Burn's found greater pleasure in good company than in the rich drawing-rooms of the New Town. He stayed in Edinburgh for only short periods spending most of the remainder of his short life in Dumfries. He died there aged thirty-seven on July 21, 1796.

There was no one quite like Robert Burns before, and none since. He was truly the most international of poets, as much loved in Russia and China as in his homeland and often claimed by other nations as their own. Today the whole world understands his poetry and his songs because they tell of things familiar to everyone. His own life was one long and losing struggle against poverty and ill-health, against the meanness of the sour earth he tilled and the threat of imprisonment for his beliefs in freedom and equality. *Scots Wha Hae* was published without his name for fear of this.

The trials of his own life gave Burns a gentle sympathy for every '. . . earth born companion an' fellow mortal', whether mouse or man, but did nothing to quench his own joy in living. And though other poets have risen to the loftiest peaks of their great art, Burns stayed where mankind lives, in the rolling plains of the ordinary people's daily toil, sharing their joy and sorrow. More than any other Scot, he spilled his genius 'the world o'er', bringing light to the minds of men and women.

Robert Burns' portrait

POEMS,

CHIEFLY IN THE

SCOTTISH DIALECT.

BY
ROBERT BURNS.

EDINBURGH:
PRINTED FOR THE AUTHOR,
AND SOLD BY WILLIAM CREECH.
M,DCC,LXXXVII.

A printing shop of the period

Worksection

The New Scots
Understand Your Work

Allan Ramsay
1 What was Edinburgh's main claim to be the 'Athens of the North'?
2 What was the sudden change that had taken place in the city that put it alongside London?
3 Where was Allan Ramsay's shop?
4 What was the shop famed for?
5 What great talent had Allan Ramsay's son?
6 How did he try to encourage learning?

David Hume and Adam Smith
1 Where, in the new town, did David Hume set up home?
2 What did he believe could be newly studied in a scientific way?
3 What modern subject grew out of his belief?
4 Why were people shocked by David Hume's book on religion?
5 How did his ideas on religion affect his career?
6 What was Adam Smith's first book called?
7 What did he warn against that mass production could cause?
8 In his view what was the true wealth of nations?
9 What new science did he invent?
10 For what particular subjects were the universities of Glasgow and Edinburgh famed?

Joseph Black and the Hunters
1 What did James Watt go to Glasgow University to do in 1756?
2 Whom did he assist there?
3 What puzzled this scientist?
4 What did he decide was happening?
5 How did Scottish thinkers and scholars spread their talents beyond Scotland?
6 What is surprising about John and William Hunter?
7 Where did they do the research work?
8 What did William Hunter give to Glasgow University?

The Adam Brothers
1 What famous buildings did James Gibbs design?
2 Who were the leading Scottish architects of the time?
3 Which of the Adam brothers was the greatest?
4 Where did he build most of his greatest masterpieces?
5 What did he design for Edinburgh's new town?

Thomas Cochrane
1 Where was Thomas Cochrane born?
2 What countries are referred to on his tomb?
3 What was he called by Napoleon?
4 Cochrane believed the war with France could be ended quickly. How?
5 What amazing feat did Cochrane perform in a sinking ship?
6 What trick did he use finally to win this battle?
7 How was Cochrane received on his return from South America?
8 What did the Speedy do when it sighted the frigate?
9 How did Cochrane trick the enemy warships?
10 Why did Cochrane not use the same tactics when he found himself close to the Gamo?
11 How did he cause the Gamo's gunners to hold their fire?
12 Why were the Spanish gunners unable to hit the Speedy with their broadside?
13 What finally won the day for the Speedy?
14 How did Cochrane earn his title 'Sea-Wolf'

Sir Walter Scott
1 What trick did Sir Walter Scott play on the public with '*Waverley*'?
2 What kind of stories did the Waverley novels contain?
3 What is the book '*Tales of a Grandfather*' about?
4 Where is Scott's monument?
5 When did Walter Scott die and in what conditions?

Robert Burns
1 When did Robert Burns first make his way to Edinburgh?
2 Where had he come from?
3 Who published Burns' first book of poems?
4 How did people react to his poetry?
5 Who published the Edinburgh edition?
6 Why do people find the things Burns wrote about easy to understand?
7 Why was '*Scots Wha Hae*' published without his name?

Use Your Imagination

1 What did David Hume mean by his reply – 'Many a better man has been made a saint o' before!'?

2 What do you think Prime Minister Pitt meant when he said to Adam Smith, 'We will stand until you are seated, for we are all your scholars'?

3 How do you think Cochrane's popularity with the Admiralty was affected by Napoleon's comment – 'If Cochrane had been supported, he would have taken every one of our ships'.

4 Why did Cochrane reckon that the Spaniards in Valdivia would not expect him to attack?

5 What forced the Admiralty to welcome and honour Cochrane on his return?

6 What kind of people do you think might not have liked the poems of Robert Burns and the views he expressed in them?

7 Robert Burns was 'the peoples' poet and he is described as the greatest of all the folk poets. What do you think is meant by this?

8 What do you suppose Burns meant when he said – 'a man's a man for a' that'?

Further Work

1 The mass production methods Adam Smith wrote about are now in general use. If, as he suggested, 'men condemned to spend their life performing a few simple operations', mindlessly and endlessly, become affected by the monotony of this experience, then you might expect unrest in industries where this happens. Do you think this is true? Check by finding out in which industries disputes, strikes and so on happen most often.

2 Can you suggest any ways to deal with such problems? Discuss this in your group and draw up a code of practice for good conditions of work and industrial relations. Remember, you still need to produce the goods. Write out your code of practice for the rest of your class to read.

3 Try to arrange a visit to Culzean Castle where you will see the work of Robert Adam and learn a good deal more about him and also about the Ayrshire country life on which Robert Burns based much of his poetry.

4 The sea adventures of C.S. Forester's '*Hornblower*' were inspired by the real life feats of Thomas Cochrane. You will enjoy reading these exciting stories, though the author felt that Cochrane's own daring and skill was more amazing than he dared make Hornblower's. People might find the truth too unbelievable even for fiction.

5 Every year in Scotland and in many countries worldwide, the birthday (25th January) of Robert Burns is celebrated at Burns Suppers. One could be organised in your class, but to do it properly you will have to learn more about the life and poems of Robert Burns and also to understand such mysteries of the menu such as 'bubbly-jock' ither, orra eattocks, and, of course, the 'great chieftain o' the puddin' race'!

When Cotton Was King

The golden years of Georgian Scotland were made possible by a huge increase in the nation's wealth. And that wealth was created by changes in the way people worked. From earliest times the Scots coaxed survival, but little comfort and fewer riches, from the unwilling land on which they stood. At the time of the Union they were still scratching only the barest living from the tired soil, often under threat of famine, rarely with anything to spare. What little manufacturing went on took place in the low dim hovels of the people at the spinning wheel and handloom. Glasgow alone flourished. Its rich tobacco lords traded with the New World. Almost forty firms exported linen cloth, thread and stockings; pottery and furniture; glass, leather and metal goods; and imported tobacco leaf; sugar and rum, hardwood and citrus fruits. The rest of the nation however, was slumped in dismal poverty.

But all this would change. Scotland's new high farming was now driving back the shadow of famine. There was food to spare and time to think. Along with the flowering of men's minds came a great new thrust of business energy and with it the endless urgent cry for greater and yet greater productivity.

Spinning

Through all of history the output of the spinners at their wheels had matched the needs of the weavers at their handlooms. But in 1733 an Englishman called John Kay made a simple change in the loom and doubled its speed. Now the weavers had to tramp many weary miles to gather enough yarn to fill their looms and, in the face of such shortage, pay high prices, even bribes, so that yarn of whatever quality they could get, would be ready in time.

The Spinning Jenny

It was during these difficult years that James Hargreaves, a weaver from Blackburn, slammed the door of his cottage in anger at the bad supply of yarn and caused his startled wife to upset her spinning wheel. It lay there its spindle still turning but now upright rather than sideways. At once Hargreaves had an idea. If a spindle could turn like this, why not a row of upright spindles all spinning yarn side by side and

Kay invented a new kind of shuttle so that the weaver no longer had to pass by hand the weft thread back and forward through the rising and falling of the warp. Instead John Kay placed the bobbin of weft in a little boat-like shuttle which sailed back and forward, riding across the lowered threads of the warp and leaving a trail of weft in its wake. It was lauched on its crossing by hammers swinging above the docking boxes at both sides and controlled by the weaver. With several of these flying shuttles, weft yarn of different colours could be ferried from separate boxes acccording to the weaving pattern. Plain and multi-coloured cloth like tartan could now be woven far quicker than ever before and the cottage spinning wheels could no longer meet the demand of the looms.

John Kay's shuttle in use

driven by one wheel. It took three years to perfect his first machine which had eight spindles. Soon this was increased to sixteen and thirty, and then more and more. Hargreaves' Spinning Jenny could make only the flimsiest cotton weft but it made this in great quantities.

Spinning now paid better than labouring in the fields. And though it was still very much a home craft, textile making was being swiftly organised as an industry by energetic businessmen with their eyes on profit.

Even the ordinary spinning wheel was much improved. Instead of the simple spindle there was now a bobbin and flyer. On to the bobbin was wound the finished yarn and it could be removed when full. And it was the flyer, twirling around the bobbin like a two pronged fork, which both spun the yarn and wound it round the bobbin. So fast did the flyer turn that to allow the yarn to be properly wound the bobbin also turned in the same direction but not at quite the same speed. The thread could then wind slowly from whirling flyer to whirling bobbin.

At her improved wheel the spinster fed the combed out fibres of wool or flax or cotton through a hole which led down the 'fork handle'. The fibres went from there out to the side and over a hook on one of the prongs before turning in and round the bobbin. Because the string that turned the bobbin could slip, the spinster was able to hold it back by pinching the fibres between her fingers. When she did this the turning of the flyer twisted and stretched them. When they were released again the finished thread wound on to the bobbin. It was the skill of the spinster which controlled how much stretch and twist each length of fibre required to become good even yarn. The idea of the bobbin and flyer was invented but not used centuries before by the great Leonardo da Vinci. And now that the wheel was treadle driven and not by hand, two such spindles were fitted to be worked one by each hand producing the better quality stronger yarn for the warp threads, at twice the speed.

The improved spinning wheel

Linen

It was linen spun and woven at home that gave Scotland her first textile industry. Next to farming, though a long way behind it, linen-making was the nation's second most important industry. All over Scotland flax was grown and linen produced. Because it was a difficult process with many stages at which to fail, the linen made was mostly a low quality coarse cloth. As the 18th century advanced, and with government aid, the industry improved and became better organised. Men like William Anderson of Banff set up business distributing flax through agents, to be spun in the homes of spinsters. The collected yarn was then sold to Mr Cox of Lochee whose family later set up the great textile industry for which Dundee came to be called 'Juteopolis'. His agents sent out the spun thread to be woven in the homes of weavers, and gathered in the finished web to be sold. At first the men like Anderson and Cox sold the raw maerials to the spinsters and weavers and bought back the finished product, but in time they became their employers, paying wages and controlling the industry. Wealth (or capital) rather than skill was now in charge. The capitalists had taken over and craftsmen would now be their dependants.

Improvements were made to the linen making process throughout that century. In 1727 a scutching machine was invented and by 1772 there were more than two hundred and fifty scutching mills. Better methods of bleaching were discovered too, but still the fibre had to be spun by hand. The gum that makes flax fibres stick together prevented the use of new machines. But another textile had come into the land, that held no such problems. The American War of Independence had suddenly cut off Glasgow's great tobacco trade so that a new major import had urgently to be found. It was cotton, and cotton would be king!

Men and women as skilled in the making of fine linen as those in Glasgow and the counties of Renfrew and Lanark would easily handle cotton. Hargreaves' Spinning Jenny could now be used and, more than that, there was another invention which would not only improve and speed up the spinning process but was best suited to cotton and would change the way the industry was organised. Indeed it would change the way the nation was organised!

Richard Arkwright

In 1769 Richard Arkwright of Preston, in the north of England, patented a new spinning machine. It had two special features. Fibres being spun need not only to be twisted but to be stretched too, and spinsters at their wheels learn by practice to judge exactly how much twist and how much stretch. The problem for the inventor was that machines could not judge tension for themselves. Hargreaves' Jenny still left the person in charge to control the amount of twist and stretch by hand. But Arkwright solved this problem.

Richard Arkwright's portrait

Flax harvesting

It was a complicated business which began with the growing of the flax plants, which, when ready, were harvested and dried. The stalks were then rotted in ponds and, when dry once more, beaten with wooden bladed knives to shed the outer layers. This was called scutching. The fibres left were combed out ready for spinning and weaving. The final product was brownish material and bleaching was needed, which could take six to eight months.

In Arkwright's spinning frame the carded (combed) and loosely twisted 'rope' of cotton fibres, called the roving, passed first through four pairs of rollers, set one after the other. Each pair was turning faster than the pair before so the roving was being drawn away from the grip of each pair of rollers quicker than it was being released. It was being stretched. Exactly how much quicker and how far apart the rollers should be and how much twisting to put in the roving in the first place were the key problems that Richard Arkwright had solved. From the last pair of rollers the now slender and even slivers of stretched cotton were spun on to the row of receiving bobbins by the whirling flyers just as on the cottage spinning wheel.

Water power

The yarn produced on Arkwright's spinning frame was a hard thread, strong enough for the warp. The other feature of his frame was that it was to be driven by water power. This it was that changed the way the nation worked. The new waterframes of Richard Arkwright had to be gathered by the riverside where fast flowing water would turn the great wheels and deliver power through driving belts to rollers and spindles. The womenfolk and children who operated the machines would work no longer in their own homes, but in the 'manufactories' or 'spinning mills'. The nearer their houses were to these factories the simpler life would be, so now a new sight was to be seen spreading over Scotland's countryside – the industrial towns. There, people would find their livelihood, not in spreading seed and reaping their modest harvest, not in the tending of flocks and herds, but by their labour in employers' factories. For this service they would be rewarded in cash. Scotland was now becoming an industrial nation. And it was happening quickly.

The first water mill was set up in 1778 on the banks of the North Esk at Penicuik, and the second, which had a thousand spindles, at Rothesay a year later. The third was on the River Levern at Neilston and the fourth, two years later in 1782 at Johnstone on the Black Cart. The 'Old End' of this mill still stands five storeys high, and is part of the modern factory where to-day Paton's laces are made. Cast iron columns support its five wooden floors. When cotton was spun there, the great driving shaft of the water

Johnstone Mill today

wheel ran the length of the mill. Upright shafts driven by gear wheels served all five floors carrying the river's power to the heart of the building and by pulley and belt to every machine in it.

Within ten years of Corse, Burns and Co. setting up that mill, five more had opened in George Houston's new town of Johnstone and over one thousand of its fourteen hundred inhabitants were mill workers. And the town was still growing, and much too fast for Houston's plans. His ideas for pleasant homes and open spaces were swept aside. Instead the crudest of miserable thatched hovels without water or sanitation crowded into the gardens or backlands of houses already there, a perfect breeding ground for cholera. But the mill owners of the new industrial age gave very little thought to the welfare of their workforce. Profit alone occupied their minds.

Child labour

And it was for the reason of profit that five year old children from the poorhouses were herded into the employment of the textile kings as orphan-apprentices, to spend long days in the great gaunt mills and nights all too brief in barrack block dormitories. Underfed and hopelessly weary they dragged their tired bodies like small sleepwalkers round and under the whirling gear wheels and flying pulley belts to where neither man nor woman could or would dare go. And if in a desperate moment's rest sleep should come, then a taskmaster's stunning blow would bring them violently to a dazed awakening, sending them once more amongst the clattering machines where the smallest slip would mean hands and arms trapped and crushed in the grinding rollers and gears. Such accidents were many but those whose labour was forced so cheaply were paid nothing when their little bodies were broken by the great machines they served, or wasted by the long unhealthy toil. The huge wealth greedily gathered by the millowners was won at an awful price.

A mill accident

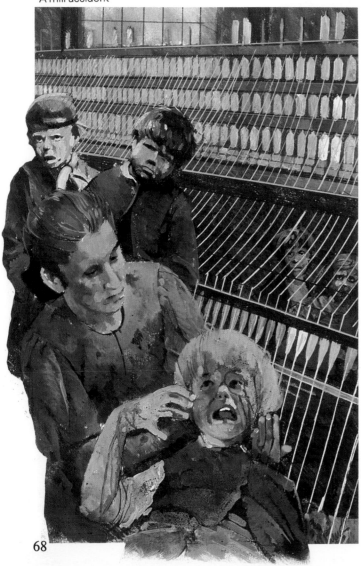

Robert Owen

Yet there was one amongst them who would not accept that profit and caring could not go together. His name was Robert Owen and he was a man ahead of his time. Owen had come from Manchester and took over in 1799 the New Lanark Mills which his father-in-law, David Dale, a Paisley weaver, had opened with Richard Arkwright. He believed completely that to make the best profit, workforce and owner must respect and trust each other. He now had his chance to test his theory.

Portrait of Robert Owen

New Lanark today showing the Mill buildings (centre and left), the 'Institute for the Formation of Character' (centre right) and the School (far right). Mill workers dwellings can be seen in the background.

A Social Experiment

At New Lanark a village of high quality, comfortable homes were offered at low rents for those families who would settle and work there. The system of orphan-apprentices, though a kindly one under David Dale, was dropped, and free modern schooling was provided. Robert Owen insisted that the children 'be taught and well trained; ... that all their instruction is rendered a pleasure and a delight to them.' The equipment for the village school included musical instruments, paste and materials for cutting and sewing, and though reading, writing, spelling and counting were thoroughly taught, music and dancing claimed an important place too. He disliked the drab old ways of teaching and set his eyes on methods that would find little use elsewhere then or for a very long time after, and in some places hardly yet! He even made sure that the books used did not hurt anyone's religious feelings. And he encouraged the old as well as the young to find benefit in education and healthy exercise.

The village store was well stocked with the best of provisions to be sold at cost price though the workers were well enough paid. Advice, which could hardly be refused, was given on the family budget. Fuel and clothing were supplied in the same way.

Robert Owen's efforts were richly rewarded. The workforce was happy and friendly and confident in the employer's good intentions. In his own words, they 'became industrious, temperate, healthy; faithful to their employer, and kind to each other; while the proprietors were deriving services from their attachment, far beyond those which could be obtained by any other means than those of mutual confidence and kindness.' He was the father of what is best in modern management and he made greater profits than those who envied him his success but clung to their backward ways. Even to-day his ideas are rarely to be found and then not always eagerly followed.

All over Scotland from the Dornoch Firth in the north to the Solway in the south spread the great new spinning mills. Now cotton really was king of the nation's trade and vast amounts of the fibre were imported to be spun and woven. Almost 70% of Scotland's export trade was in cotton cloth.

Steam

Samuel Crompton's Spinning Mule which was a mixture of Hargreaves' jenny and Arkwright's water-frame was now in use, and something else too. For the first time a new force was to turn the cotton spindles, not muscle, wind or water but the thumping hissing energy of steam. The great fire-engines of James Watt's inventive genius were now harnessed to the driving shafts of the spinning mills. Coal rather than fast flowing water was the mill's life blood and Glasgow now became the centre of the cotton trade. By 1831 three quarters of Scotland's 192 mills were either within the city itself or close by in Paisley.

Weaving too was now becoming power driven and the rich days of the well-to-do weaver working his four day week in his own cottage were suddenly at an end. Weaving was just another factory job, automatic and no longer well paid, except in Paisley. There the high skill of the hand weavers produced Scotland's proudest and finest textile pattern – the wondrous flow of intricate multicoloured commas and leaves of the world famous Paisley Pattern Shawls. And it was in Paisley too that J. and P. Coats, the world leaders in the spinning of sewing thread first set up their mill in 1835. They employed only one hundred and fifty then but by 1914 the workforce in their mighty mills at Ferguslie and Anchor was ten thousand strong.

Paisley patterned shawl *c*1830

A steam mill interior

Power

By 1840 more than a quarter of a million Scots worked in the great cotton mills of the west and in Dundee's thriving jute and flax business, in the making of Dunfermline's fine linens and in the woollen trade, weaving the tartan cloth and soft border tweeds that Sir Walter Scott's tales of Jacobite adventure had made popular. Fully one tenth of the whole nation were textile workers. Yet this was not simply the age of cotton and flax and wool, it was the age of iron and coal too. Black riches were dug from the deep earth, to build and fuel a new industrial Scotland.

Coal

From the beginning the coal industry had been a moderate one. It was restricted to surface scraping wherever outcrops were to be found. There were shallow bell pits too, little more than shafts widened at the foot and sometimes extended by cutting 'rooms' in the seam, leaving pillars (stoops) of uncut coal to support the roof. How deep and how large a mine could be was limited not by how much coal there was, but by bad drainage and bad ventilation and the risk of exploding fire-damp (methane gas).

By the middle of the eighteenth century when Culloden Field was being bitterly contested, shafts were reaching down almost eighty metres. It was beyond the depth which could be emptied of flood-water by the methods then in use: endless chains of wooden buckets hoisted to the surface by great water or horse driven wheels called 'gins' and, in some places, pumps driven by Thomas Newcomen's steam engines. Half a million tons of Scottish coal were dug out in a year and transported from the pit heads by small cart and pack horse to be burned in the family hearth, in the boiling down of salt, in lime burning, and in glass making.

Apart from farms and mills, Scotland's coal mines were soon employing more labour than any other industry. Most miners were bound for life to the pit owner as serfs, almost slaves, unable ever to leave their master. The methods they used to win the coal had remained unchanged over the centuries.

At the pit head, and (**above**) a contemporary view

The miners

Scotland's pit owners had nothing to learn from their mill owning friends about the business of forcing cheap labour from weary children, many of whom were yoked to the coal pit even at their christening, to be serfs for all the days of their lives. Nor did the owners miss any chance to tighten their grasp on the men of the workforce. Company stores were set up, not of course as Robert Owen had done to help his workers, but to trap the miners into debt. Goods at the highest possible prices were sold on credit terms. Wages were only paid out after the bill had been settled which left very little in the pay packet. More credit was needed almost at once and the miner was held fast in a web of debt unable even to shop around for better value.

Cross-section through Gilmerton Colliery 1786, near Edinburgh, one of the earliest illustrations of a Scottish coal mine.

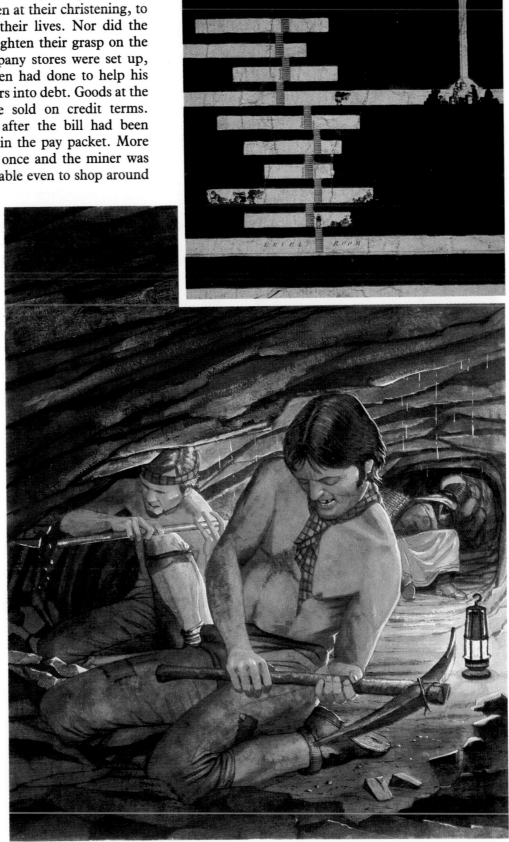

Squatting awkwardly in the black damp of the tunnels the hewer swung his pick in low sideways sweeps to hack a deep slot at the base of the seam. Even if standing upright undercutting like this would be hard enough, but cramped there in a space barely half the height of a man the work was doubly exhausting. Only the arms and twisting of the waist could swing the pick. There was no help from the legs. Breathing, always difficult in the foul heat of the pit, was then harder still.

Above the slot, the hewer drove wedges into the coal to burst down a section of wall face. The broken coal was then loaded into a basket creel to be heaved onto the bent back of a bearer and there held by the tug straps which passed round the forehead. The loaded creel weighed as much as a fully grown man (over seventy kilos) and was borne by the stooping, staggering bearer along the low tunnels and up several long ladders to the shaft bottom. There the coal was dumped into a tub which, when filled, would be hoisted to the surface by the pit-head gin. Four of these back breaking journeys would fill only one tub. Always the bearer was female, often a nine or ten year old girl and she would fill five tubs in her fourteen or sixteen hour shift, working for her father who cut the coal.

James Watt's Invention

By the end of the century, Scotland's industries were demanding more and more coal and her growing population, now approaching two million, burned increasing amounts in their home fires. At Kinneil near Bo'ness, in 1768, a new engine was constructed at the Burn Pit. With its great see-saw beam and boiler, its hissing steam and sliding rods it looked very much like a Newcomen engine. But this one was different. It was James Watt's. His time with Dr. Black at Glasgow University had been well remembered and he knew that a great deal of heat was used up when boiling water turned to steam. Dr. Black had called it 'Latent Heat' because it did not register on the thermometer.

But James Watt did more. He improved his engines and fitted them to turn wheels. No longer were they steam pumps, now he had invented the rotary engine with the piston driven by steam in both directions. Soon the cotton spindles of Scotland (and England) twirled to the power of steam, and the great mills settled in large towns, Glasgow and Paisley, without the need to be near fast flowing water.

right: Portrait of James Watt

below: Newcomen and Watt's pumping engines

Both engines, Newcomen's and Watt's, worked in the same general way. Air was driven out of a cylinder by filling it with steam. Then the steam was quickly cooled to condense it into a few drops of water. This process caused a vacuum which brought the piston down the cylinder, pushed by the pressure of air outside which was trying to fill the vacuum. The piston pulled down one end of the 'See-saw' beam, lifting the other end with it, the pump shaft. When the vacuum was released by a valve, down went the heavy pump shaft and as the beam tipped the other way, up came the piston sucking in more steam to be condensed so all this would happen again.

In Thomas Newcommen's engine the whole business took place inside the cylinder which meant, of course, that the cylinder was hot when it should have been cold to condense the steam, and cold when it should have been hot to receive the new steam without condensing it before it had filled the cylinder. Heat and fuel were wasted by this problem. Watt solved it by producing a separate consenser for the steam. Now the cylinder could be kept at steam heat and the condenser properly chilled. The opening and shutting of valves allowed the steam to be sucked from the hot cylinder into the cold condenser, leaving behind the vacuum to bring down the piston. It was a much more efficient system.

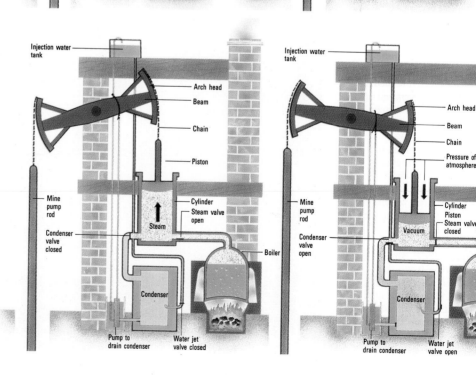

New Mining Methods

With such pit-head engines to pump out floodwater and hoist heavy loads to the surface, coal could now be cut from deeper seams and the huge demand could be met. In less than half a century coal production had grown five-fold to two and a half million tons by 1810, and it was rising more steeply all the time. Better methods were employed underground. No longer was the wasteful 'room and pillar' in general use, leaving uncut a third of the precious coal to bear the weight of the roof. Extra shafts were sunk to improve ventilation in the long deep galleries and a system of doors or traps directed the flow of fresher air through all parts of the mine.

Working Conditions

At Culross in 1793, the earl of Dundonald, father of the Sea Wolf, Cochrane, abolished all underground labour for women and girls in his mines. Instead, pit ponies drew the truckloads of coal along the wooden rails of the waggon ways. He also did away with the debt trap of the company store. But, for the East of Scotland, the Earl was unusual. There life below the ground would continue to be a grim affair, shared by little girls and their mothers until in the middle of the nineteenth century (1842) when a law was passed against female labour. By then the serfdom of the miners had also been ended by Acts of Parliament in 1775 and 1779. Slavery in Scotland was finally abolished, less then two hundred years ago.

In the west, things were never quite so bad for the mine workers. Females were not employed underground and by 1820 the miners had united together to protect their living standards. The owners, always on the look-out for cheap labour, replied by bringing in Irish labourers at lower rates of pay. There was a long and angry struggle between employer and unions. Most of the Irish workforce were Catholics and so, even when the labour troubles were settled, a bitter religious tension lingered on in the Protestant west of Scotland. There had been real enough reasons at the beginning for strife: falling wages and lower living conditions. Yet, though the quarrel is now an empty one, it has not completely died even today.

Charcoal Burning

Until half way through the eighteenth century the iron-makers of Scotland (and England) had no great use for coal. They smelted the ore to bring out the metal using charcoal and it was the charcoal burners who prepared the fuel for the furnaces. They spent

First the timber was felled and trimmed to even lengths. These were stacked upright in circular heaps. Then the whole cone-shaped pile was covered in turf and packed with earth or ash. Through a hole at the top burning wood was inserted to set the timber inside slowly smouldering in the feeble air flow from small openings round the base.

their days and nights camped in the forest clearings, preparing the timber fires which produced the charcoal; a very different life from the miner in his deep foul galleries.

Throughout the long slow burn the men watched their smoking mounds carefully in case too much air should enter and set the pile ablaze. When at last all the wood had been turned to charcoal and was cool enough it was broken out ready to fuel the smelting furnaces. The charcoal produced was only a quarter of the weight of the wood which had been burned and Scotland's forests were fast disappearing before the advance of the charcoal burners.

The iron masters of Scotland, and England too, spread out through the wild hillsides of the northern kingdom. They took their ore with them and lit their fires wherever the supply of charcoal timber was good enough: at Invergarry, Taynuilt and Inveraray, at Bonawe and Furnace, and at Abernethy too.

Iron Works

But the wild search for charcoal came to an end when Abraham Darby's method for smelting ore with coal was learned. Now iron foundry and coal mine would be partners. Now the iron industry demanded coal as it had once demanded forests.

North of Falkirk, famed then for its mighty Cattle Trysts (when in the autumn the highland droves brought the great herds south to the market), there now appeared a strange apparatus. On the banks of the River Carron two hollow towers, fourteen metres high and built of masonry bound with iron hoops, were constructed among other buildings and sheds. Near the base of each massive cone there was a pipe to which was attached four gigantic bellows powered by a large water wheel. The mighty strokes of the bellows sent shuddering blasts of air roaring deep into the heart of the fire that raged within. With every blast great spurts of wild fire were thrust high above the stack. And at six hour intervals men would rush to tend their fire monsters, releasing a bright flow of molten metal from the base along grooves formed in a bed of sand. The main channel was called the sow and the short branches all along each side were the pigs. At the Carron Iron Works Scotland's iron masters lit their first blast furnace to smelt pig iron. They used not charcoal but coal, and of that Scotland had plenty.

Weapons and Tools

Coal was not put 'raw' into the smelting fires. Instead it was smouldered in ovens to make coke which was mixed with lime and iron ore to charge the blast furnaces at Carron. By 1767 there were four, and the first of the new James Watt engines was set up there to pump water for the wheel that drove the bellows. They produced the iron for the machines of war that the Duke of Wellington required for his long campaign against Napoleon. The huge yard at Falkirk was 'covered with cannons, mortars, bombs, balls, and those large pieces, short and expanded at the breech, which bear the name of "carronades". Amidst these machines of war, these terrible instruments of death, gigantic cranes, capstans of every kind, levers and assemblages of pulleys, serving to move so many heavy loads, are erected . . .'

A Carron gun (of about 1800) or carronade

And Wellington, writing from Freneda on 9th October, 1811, specially demanded guns from this firm and no other. 'I have had enough of sieges with defective artillery and I will never undertake another without the best. Therefore in all my letters I have desired to have either 29 pcs. 9 feet long Carron manufacture, or 29 pcs. 8 feet long of the same manufacture and Carron shot.' And HMS *Victory*, Flagship of Admiral Lord Nelson at Trafalgar, carried cannon from the same factory.

Iron-making followed coal-mining and spread fast across the narrow waist of Scotland. By 1801 there were nine iron-works in the counties of Lanark, Ayr and Fife and the market for iron was growing: not just for weapons of war but to be beaten into ploughshares to serve the new high farming. Twenty-nine blast furnaces fanned by James Watt engines, poured out in a glowing stream more than twenty thousand tons of pig iron in a year.

Neilson's 'Hot-Blast'

But the young iron industry had its problems and growth was slowing down. Scottish coal produced coke at a high price. England and Wales could make iron cheaper. Then quite suddenly in 1828, James Beaumont Neilson, born in Shettleston and manager of the Glasgow Gas Works, had an idea. He noticed that while fresh cold air was blasted into the furnace, very hot gas was escaping from the top. The fire was being cooled and fuel wasted keeping up the heat. Instead Neilson capped the top of the stack and took the roasting hot gases down again by pipe to heat the air before it was blasted in. With the new hot-blast, not only could raw coal be used instead of expensive coke, but Scotland's rich supplies of Blackband iron-stone, which had been discovered by David Muchet, twenty-seven years before, could now be smelted. The iron stone was a mixture of coal and ore, and pig iron could now be drawn from it by the new furnaces for less than one third of the previous cost. At once the picture changed. New iron-works sprang up on the Monklands of Lanarkshire where coal and ironstone were in rich supply: Bairds of Gartsherrie, Wilson of Dundyvan, and at Summerlee too, all by Coatbridge. And in 1839 William Dixon lit his famous 'Blazes' at Govanhill in Glasgow.

Within twelve years of Neilson's invention Scotland's ironmasters had four times as many furnaces in blast. They had increased production from less than forty thousand tons in a year to more than two hundred and forty thousand tons. And the increase would go on. By 1860 a million tons were smelted in the hundred and seventy-one furnaces. Central Scotland was now producing a quarter of all Britain's pig iron.

Neilson's blast furnace

The Price

But such a growth had to be paid for. It left deep scars on the life and landscape of Scotland. The ironmasters showed no more concern for the welfare of their workforce and the quality of its dwelling places than did the mill and pit owners. In their minds too, the dream of profit left little room for other thoughts. By night iron towns like Motherwell and Coatbridge were an awesome sight, their skies ablaze with the red fire of the great works. But by day they were drab dismal places crouched under rolling banks of smoke from tall chimneys; mean grey places, unhealthy and over-crowded with the usual huddle of unsanitary company housing, grasping company stores and, in Gartsherrie at least, a company church, all blackened by the falling soot.

James Watt's great engines gave to industrial Scotland her heart and muscle with which to pump out the deep mines and raise coal for her fires, to power the machines of her factories. The 'hot-blast' of James Beaumont Neilson made possible the vast supply of iron on which the nation soon depended. And the great Welshman Robert Owen brought conscience and caring into this new iron-hard age of blazing furnace and deafening machinery, of gaunt mill and foul pit.

Worksection

Understand Your Work
When Cotton Was King

Spinning
1 What made possible the new developments of Georgian Scotland?
2 What happened in 1733 that made it difficult for weavers to find enough yarn for their looms?
3 What part of the loom did John Kay alter?
4 How did James Hargreaves get the idea for his new invention?
5 What quality of yarn could the jenny produce?
6 What name is given to the thread which the shuttle carries?
7 Who invented the idea of the bobbin and flyer?
8 What effect did driving the wheel by foot have on spinning?
9 Which yarn has to be stronger, weft or warp?

Linen
1 What was the country's second most important industry?
2 Why was the linen of a coarse, low quality?
3 How was this improved?
4 What city was called 'Juteopolis' and why?
5 What important change in the control of textile making began to take place?
6 What effect did this have on the craftsmen?
7 What does scutching mean?
8 What ended the Glasgow tobacco trade?
9 What was the new textile which was now imported?
10 How did this suit the spinning jenny?

Richard Arkwright and Water Power
1 Why was it difficult to invent a spinning machine?
2 How was the cotton stretched on Arkwright's frame?
3 What quality of thread was produced on Arkwright's spinning frame?
4 In what other way was it different from the spinning jenny?
5 How did this influence where they were constructed?
6 What now happened instead of working at home?
7 How did this influence where houses were built?
8 In what way was the working life of the Scottish nation now changing?
9 Where and when did it all begin in Scotland?
10 How was the power of the flowing water harnessed to work the spinning frames?
11 What happened to George Houston's plans for Johnstone?
12 What was the main interest of the mill owners at this time?

Robert Owen and a Social Experiment
1 How did the mill owners treat young children?
2 What dangers did the children face?

3 What care was taken of the victims of accidents?
4 What did Robert Owen think about the practices of his fellow industrialists?
5 What did he believe was the right relationship between workforce and owner?
6 What did he say that all instruction should be?
7 What was special about the village store?
8 Did his system work?

Steam
1 What was entirely new about Crompton's mule?
2 How did this alter the placing of new mills?
3 What other part of the textile trade now took place in factories?
4 How did Paisley resist this change?
5 When did J & P Coats begin to manufacture thread?

Power

Coal
1 Where were the great textile centres of Scotland?
2 How many people were employed in the industry?
3 What else played a big part in Scottish industry apart from textiles?
4 What limited the depth and size of a coal mine?
5 How were coal miners treated by the owners?
6 How did this system affect children?
7 What difference was there between the pit owners' shops and Robert Owen's store?
8 What made digging coal doubly difficult?
9 How and by whom was the coal removed from the coal face and taken to the surface?

James Watt's Invention
1 How did the original steam engines work?
2 What did Watt decide was wrong with this design?
3 What did he do to improve matters?
4 What other improvement did he make?
5 How did this affect the mills?

New Mining Methods and Working Conditions
1 How did Watt's new steam pump and rotary engine affect mining?
2 How much coal was dug out in 1810 in Scotland?
3 How much of the coal was left in the 'room and pillar' mine to hold the roof?
4 How was the ventilation in the mines improved?
5 What did the Earl of Dundonald do to improve things in his mines at Culross in 1793?
6 How long did it take the other east coast mines to end female labour?
7 When was serfdom finally abolished in Scotland?
8 Why did the miners unite in the west of Scotland?
9 What did the owners do when this union was formed?
10 What lasting effect did this action cause?

Charcoal Burning

1 About when did they begin to use coal for smelting?
2 What was used before then?
3 How was it produced?
4 What are some of the places the charcoal burners visited?
5 What was it the charcoal burners had to prevent happening to the smouldering pile?

Ironworks, Weapons and Tools

1 Whose discovery ended the use of charcoal for smelting?
2 What new link was forged between industries?
3 What had Falkirk been famed for before the founderies came?
4 What was a blast furnace?
5 Why was the iron called pig iron?
6 Why was Scotland a good country in which to smelt iron by the new method?
7 How was coal prepared for the blast furnaces?
8 Who ordered weapons from Carron Iron Works?
9 Why did he insist on the products of the Falkirk firm?
10 What else was manufactured at the iron works?

Neilson's Hot-Blast and The Price

1 When did Neilson invent the hot-blast?
2 What was wrong with using cold air to fan the furnace?
3 What benefits did his invention have for the Scottish iron industry?
4 By 1860 how much iron was produced in a year?
5 Were the iron industry employers any better than the pit or mill owners?
6 What effect did the growth of the iron industry have on the lives of the people?
7 What did Robert Owen bring to the new industrial Scotland?

Use Your Imagination

1 Why do you think it might be said that the new farming methods made the new industries possible?

2 Why was spinning now attracting people away from work on the farms, do you think?

3 Why do you think people accepted the terrible conditions of factory and mine working?

4 Why do you suppose they did not object to the heartless treatment of the children?

5 What do you imagine Robert Owen's fellow mill owners thought of him?

6 Do you think Owen introduced all his new ideas just to make more money?

7 Faced with the terrible conditions of work in most mills, foundries and mines, how do you think the work force could try to get a better deal?

8 What effect do you imagine the use of charcoal for smelting had on Scotland's countryside?

9 What effect do you suppose the use of coal had on the mining industry?

10 How would the use of coal for smelting affect the choice of sites for iron works?

Further Work

1 Not every one of Robert Owen's workers was happy with the way of life at New Lanark. Discuss, in your group, why this might be so.

Now divide your group into two halves. One half should imagine that they are discontented workers at New Lanark and write letters to Owen saying why they want to leave.

The other half should then write replies explaining why this is a bad idea and what benefits would be lost by moving to another mill.

2 Two hundred years ago iron was too dear for ordinary people to buy very much. What tools would a cottager need who owns some land, too small for a plough? Discuss this in your group and make a list.
Tools can be made more easily and cheaply from wood but they wear out quickly. Your group's task now is to improve the wooden tools using the least amount possible of iron. Make models of your tools with cardboard etc. and use kitchen foil to show where you would use the iron. Display your models with captions for the class to see.

3 Here is the beginning of a play called '*The Wrong Decision*'.

Scene: Outside a simple drift mine.

Jake	Right lads. Into the hole again and let's get on with it. What's wrong with you, George, hanging back with a face like fizz?
George	No, nothing . . . but . . .
Walter	Go on, George, tell him.
George	Well, Jake, as a matter of fact, we think we've dug far enough. We don't think we should go any further.
Jake	Eh? Far enough! Aw c'm on! That's the best coal we've ever had. No stone in it. And easy to hew. We can't stop now!
Robbie	What's wrong with you two anyway? Scared of the dark?
George	No. I'm not scared, Robbie – and you watch your tongue. But we're digging down. What if we hit water? And there's the roof. We don't think the roof's safe.
Walter	Aye, there was that stuff that fell yesterday . . .
Robbie	Huh! Pebbles! Just dirt and some pebbles.
Jake	That's all it was, right enough. Still . . . what do the rest of you think?

Pick 'actors' in your class to read through the play. Continue the play with others including the women who carry the coal joining in the argument for and against digging further. You decide to go ahead and it is the wrong decision. What happens? Act out the story and finish the play.

Tradeways

When the Georgian years ended with the death of George IV in 1830, the kingdom in the north was already an industrial one. Scotland now rang, not to the sound of the woodman's axe, but to the din of the forge master's hammer. But it was not only coal and cotton, ironstone and steampower that had made possible the change from farmstead and country craft to great town and heavy industry, from open field to factory floor. Without a developing transport system none of this could have happened. Neither could the coal and ore have reached the furnace, nor the finished goods their customers.

The State of the Roads

Until quite late in the eighteenth century Scotland's roads were so bad that they kept apart the towns and burghs they should have joined. In dry weather the ruts and boulders quickly jolted to pieces the few carts which used them. In the frequent Scottish rain they were turned into tracks of soft mud in which wheels sank axle-deep. The poor road transport there also cost dearly. For coal carted the twelve or so miles from the Monklands pits around Coatbridge to Glasgow, customers were charged double the pit head price. And in the east, the eighty mile round trip between Selkirk and Edinburgh could take two weeks. And the easiest part of the route was wading along the shallow bed of Gala Water! Overland travel in Scotland was a desperate business barely suited to foot and hoof and almost impossible for wheeled vehicles. Pack horse and river were still the only real means of transport.

Tollhouse at Kinkell Bridge, Perthshire, c1760

Turnpike Trusts

There were, of course, the Highland roads and bridges of General Wade including his lovely five arched span over the Rivery Tay at Aberfeldy. But they were constructed after the Jacobite uprising of 1715 and were designed for military use. The same was true of those built after the 'Forty-Five rebellion. Neither network served the trade routes of the new industrial Scotland.

In 1751 the Government at Westminster took a hand in the matter. It granted to groups of private people the right to charge fees for use of roads which they would improve and repair. About three hundred and fifty of these groups, or 'turnpike trusts' as they were called, were formed during the next ninety years or so, by important local people: men of business, landowners and the like. Dotted all along the roadways there appeared little toll houses with spiked gates to bar the way and make sure that the tolls were paid. The spikes, for which the roads were called turnpikes, were there to discourage riders who would rather jump the gate than pay the toll or perhaps, if they were highwaymen, would rather not be delayed or recognised.

In Ayrshire the roads laid by the turnpike trusts gave the county a system which is still used today – though with modern surfacing. Amongst the members of an Ayrshire trust was one of the two Scots who would give Britain and the whole world the modern science of roadmaking. His name was John Loudon McAdam.

New Systems of Roadmaking

Now road laying took on a quite different look. Instead of gangs of roadmen swinging great sledge hammers to smash huge stones, women and old men sat amongst piles of clean drystone or flints, tapping away with long shafted light hammers. They were making small sharp broken stones. The stones had to be no larger than would fit in the mouth of the stonebreaker. Instead of filling potholes with large boulders or laying heavy stone blocks for foundations, the road gang carefully prepared a bed of firm dry soil raised higher in the middle and curving down to both sides. Then a ditch was dug all along each edge. On the surface of the road-bed a twenty-five centimetre layer of the broken stone was carefully spread, the smallest stones on top. This done, the work of the roadmen was finished. The iron-clad wheels of coach and cart did the rest, grinding the small stones to dust and packing it down on to the larger ones below. The ground stone sealed the road surface and made it rainproof. The camber shed the water into the ditches where it drained it away, so that it could not seep between the soil and the stone cover. No water could reach the road bed and soften its firm foundation.

By giving the simple beaten track a hard wearing raincoat John Loudon McAdam produced a first class road that improved the more it was used. Extra layers of small stones were added for the traffic to grind in and further strengthen the surface. The McAdam roads were self repairing. He described his method like this:

McAdam gave two new words to the language – 'macadamised' which means made by the McAdam method, and 'tarmac' or 'tarmacadam' which means a McAdam road to which tar is added to prevent modern rubber tyres sucking out the sealing stone-dust and spoiling the raincoat.

above: cross-section through a McAdam road and (**left**) a portrait of John Loudon McAdam

'As no artificial road can be made so good as the natural soil in a *dry state*, it is necessary to preserve this state. The first operation should be the reverse of digging a trench. The road should not be sunk below, but raised above, the adjacent ground; that there be a sufficient fall to take off the water, so that it should be some inches below the level of the ground upon which the road is, either by making the drains to lower ground or, if that be not practicable from the nature of the country, then the soil upon which the road is laid, must be raised some inches above the level of the water.

Having secured the soil from *under* water, the road-maker is next to secure it from rain-water, by a solid road, of clean, dry stone, or flint, so selected, prepared and laid, as to be impervious to water; and this cannot be affected, unless the greatest care be taken, that no earth, clay, chalks, or other matter, that will hold water, be used with the broken stone; which must be so laid, as to unite by its own angles into a firm, compact, impenetrable body.'

Thomas Telford

The other great road builder was Thomas Telford. His methods were more expensive than McAdam's. Telford laid a solid foundation of carefully cut and fitted stone blocks on the well drained road bed. Above this there was a layer of medium stones and then a top coat of gravel to smooth and seal the surface, and to make it less harmful to the hooves of horse and cattle.

But Telford was more than a road builder; he was among the very greatest civil engineers in a great age of engineers. In 1803 he was invited by the Government to look in to the special difficulties of the Highlands and, as a result of the report he prepared, he was given the task of carrying out the work. Under his direction and despite the endless problems of a rugged unwilling landscape, a dour unwilling Highland workforce and unwilling paymasters in Westminster, more than nine hundred miles of good road and more than eleven hundred bridges were completed by 1820. They were beautiful bridges, like those spanning the Tay at Dunkeld and the Spey at Craigellachie, like Bonar Bridge over the headwaters of the Dornoch Firth and Spean Bridge in Inverness-shire; all different but all touched with Telford's engineering artistry.

Telford's bridge spanning the Tay at Dunkeld

Passengers and Mail

The work and example of McAdam and Telford transformed the roads of all Britain. By the mid 1830s a huge passenger and mail service covered the whole country. Three thousand coaches with a hundred and fifty thousand horses plied the turnpikes of Britain, Europe's finest roads. Now by mail express London, which before 1780 was a month's hard travel from Edinburgh, was within two and a half days. Coaches out of Edinburgh and Glasgow ran to Stirling, Aberdeen, Dumfries, Carlisle, London and on Telford's new roads, north to Inverness and the Highlands; in fact, all over the kingdom.

Scotland now resounded to beating hooves and cracking whips, rumbling wheels and rattling harness of flying swaying coaches as they swept along the new highways. The air was split by the urgent blare of the post horns warning the toll-keeper to open his gate or the next posting inn to have fresh horses ready. A quick change, and the coach would be off again, clattering out of the inn yard and on down the highway on the next stage of the journey. And they raced each other, the rival companies, side by side and neck and neck, the drivers urging on their teams and the coaches pitching and swinging dangerously close, as one inched past the other. The best service was the fastest service.

It was a hard way to travel, even on the new turnpike roads of McAdam and Telford. Passengers who braved the outside seats could be thrown from the speeding coach or risk freezing to death in the bitter winter weather. Coaches were sometimes lost in the snow, horses were often driven too hard and rarely lasted more than two years on stage coach service.

The Navigators

But it was not the roads with their heavy tolls that carried the great loads of lime and marl to the farmlands or coal and ore to the iron works; the iron cannon and steam engine to the customer and bales of cotton cloth to the docks. Another form of transport would bear these great burdens, and already people's interest was growing in the new work being done all around them.

First came the men with the rolled up plans and measuring chains, the sighting telescopes and the tall striped staffs. They were the surveyors and engineers. They talked earnestly, pointing here and there, consulting their maps and plans. Pegs and posts were hammered in to mark out a route and then the men moved on. Later came the work gangs. Hundreds of men with picks and shovels, barrows and carts. Gradually a great 'navigation' or trench was opened, twenty metres across at the top, half the width at the bottom and cut exactly to the route markers.

Again and again the surveyors checked the line and level, for the trench bottom had to be dead level and the line as straight as possible. If rock got in the way it was blasted aside. If the ground rose, it was cut through or pierced with a tunnel. If it fell, then a bank or bridge was built. And if the hill was too long then the trench was carried over it in steps, each dead level, a staircase up one side and down the other as it cut its way through farmland and moor, coalfield and iron works.

Then, all along the route men applied a thick coating of softened clay to the dry sides and bottom, for they had to be made waterproof. Flood water that interfered with the work was drained away, or pumped out by the mighty beam engines of James Watt. The 'steps' of the great 'staircases' had vertical sides held firm by stone walling, and fitted to front and rear, there were massive timber doors. The steps too, had to hold water.

When, at last, after years of digging and building the long, long trench was ready and the engineers were satisfied, it was flooded with water from river and reservoir, section by section, end to end.

To mark the great day a boat would then sail the whole length of the man made river, watched by cheering crowds and bands playing. The new waterway would then be ready, joining one part of Scotland to another: river to river, ironworks to coalfield, to city, to port; a new form of transport for the nation – the canal.

It was a natural enough idea for the northern kingdom where the river had long been the best highway. Water travel was cheap and convenient if the waterways happened to run to the proper places. For this reason Scottish towns over the centuries, had grown up by the sea, on the lochside and on the riverbank. But the new industries and high farming demanded transport along routes not followed by natural waterways. The answer to this problem in the minds of the courageous Georgians had been simple enough. The water would be made to flow where it was needed. Canals would now carry the heavy burdens for the new industrial Scotland.

A canal under construction

The Engineers

The surveying, design and construction of Scotland's canals were put in the hands of the great engineers: James Watt and Thomas Telford, John Smeaton and John Rennie. Smeaton had designed the lighthouse that was to guard the lone Eddystone rock for more than a century, and it is his slender bridge that still spans the Tay at Perth. It was Rennie who built Waterloo Bridge in London and carried the road over the Tweed at Kelso on five wide arches. These men brought all their energy, art and genius to the age of the canal.

The Forth and Clyde canal

In the summer of 1769 work began in the mud flats at the mouth of the Grange Burn where it joins the River Carron to flow into the Firth of Forth. From there a thousand men directed by John Smeaton drove the Forth and Clyde Canal across the waist of Scotland. The thirty-nine miles of canal with as many locks were not completed until 1790 when it joined the Clyde on its north bank at Bowling.

The money for the project was first put up by the tobacco merchants of Glasgow. When their trade collapsed about 1777 work stopped. Eventually further money was provided from public funds to finish the job. A branch down into what is now the heart of Glasgow was opened about the same time as the main route, and there the busy harbour of Port Dundas was built by Sir Lawrence Dundas. The eastern end of the canal passed through his lands at Kerse and there Dundas set up a small township for the profit he would collect in rents. It was sited between the Grange Burn and the River Carron close by the gates of the great sealock. At first the township was called Sea Lock. Today it is the premier port on the east coast of Scotland and, since 1784, has been better known as Grangemouth.

Other branches were added to the canal: at Glasgow to carry coal the twelve miles from the Monklands pits to the city; at Falkirk, to serve the great Carron Iron Works. By 1808, eighty thousand tons of coal were carried in a single year on the barges of the Forth and Clyde Canal. Herring boats switched coasts through it. There were passenger services too. By 1817 profits were good and the public now enjoyed cheaper transport and cheaper goods. Glasgow no longer had to pay double the pit head prices for its coal from the Monklands. The Forth and Clyde was the first and most important of the Scottish canals. Soon a whole network of canals was constructed to serve similar purposes.

Some Failures

Not all the canals were successfully completed. An exciting scheme to join Glasgow with a new port at Ardrossan on the Ayrshire coast stopped short at Johnstone in 1810 when the money ran out. It was a first class waterway carried ten metres high over the River Cart at Blackhall in Paisley, on an aqueduct almost eighty metres long and through two tunnels of about the same length, further west in Paisley. It ended abruptly in the harbour basin by the foot of Thorn Brae in Johnstone. The canal was struck by disaster shortly after its opening when on Saturday, 10th November 1810, a barge overloaded with trippers overturned in the Paisley basin early in the afternoon. Amid the panic and confusion eighty-five people drowned in the six feet of water and sixty of them were children.

The Firth and Clyde canal today

The Caledonian Canal

But the proudest engineering feat of that proud age of canal building took place far to the north of Scotland's new industrial heartland, in the wild and rugged Highland landscape of the Great Glen. It was Thomas Telford's mighty Caledonian Canal. Both Watt and Telford had surveyed and reported on the best route and in 1803 the work began. A channel was driven from the headwaters of Loch Linnhe in the west to the Moray Firth away to the north-east. Sixty miles of waterway joined the Atlantic Ocean to the North Sea.

It was a daunting task. Twenty-three miles of canal, thirty metres wide were required to join Loch Linnhe to Loch Lochy to Loch Oich and on to black Loch Ness, finally breaking through to the Firth. There was dredging to do, and twenty-nine locks to build including what was then the largest in the world. And all this against brooding landscape, bleak hostile weather and the unending shortage of supplies and materials. It took a workforce, three thousand strong, twenty years to complete the huge labour. At last on Monday, 23rd October 1822 to the loud salute of guns and the stirring blare of the Inverness Militia Band, a ship left Muirtown on the Moray Firth, on the maiden passage along the great waterway. Through the sixty miles of manmade channel and sheersided loch that now split the Great Glen, the little steamship made its historic progress. Finally it descended the eight locks of 'Neptune's Staircase' from Loch Lochy and on into Fort William, to cheering crowds and blazing bonfires. The Caledonian Canal cost more than a million pounds to build and was never able to show a profit, but it remains today Scotland's finest monument to the genius of Thomas Telford and perhaps the loveliest working waterway in the world.

Deepening the River

There was yet another problem for these great engineers to solve. Glasgow merchants, for all their wealth and success, were still compelled to use downriver ports. Late in the eighteenth century the Clyde was still a wide lazy river, whose banks were the meadowland on which cattle grazed amongst the shrubs of broom, and women did their laundry amid their paddling children. Only the smallest craft could come upriver to the city and the cargo ships and their docks were more than sixteen miles away at Port Glasgow.

In 1768 the City fathers consulted John Golborne of Chester about deepening the shallow river. He proposed a system of jetties to alter the flow so that a deep channel would be scoured by the river itself. The scheme was a success and later work by Watt, Rennie and Telford further improved the channel. By 1830 the Clyde in Glasgow was almost 5 metres deep at high water. Now Glasgow was its own port and the money flowed in. The once pleasant river side was disfigured and blackened with quayside and dockland, warehouse and shipyard. What had been lazy shallows were now turned into Scotland's most important riverway, carrying by 1830, a million tons of shipping in a year. The pleasant shrubs and the peaceful meadowland of Clydeside were now remembered only in the names 'Broomielaw' and 'Meadowside', by which the quays are still known today.

Clydeside today looking downstream past Meadowside

The Ports

And it was not only within the kingdom that the engineers were busy, but at its gateways too. The ports now received attention, and harbours were extended or rebuilt. By Telford at Aberdeen and along the north-east coastline, and elsewhere by Smeaton, Rennie and the Stevensons who also won greater fame as lighthouse builders. It was Robert and his sons who now ringed Scotland's dangerous coasts with their tall flashing beacons to light the way for the seafarers, to and from the new harbours with their cargoes. Robert Stevenson's grandson also began training as a civil engineer but soon turned to other things. He lit a quite different kind of light. His vivid, exciting adventure stories: *Kidnapped* and *Treasure Island* and the sinister tale of *The Strange Case of Dr. Jekyll and Mr. Hyde*, made Robert Louis Stevenson the leading writer of his time.

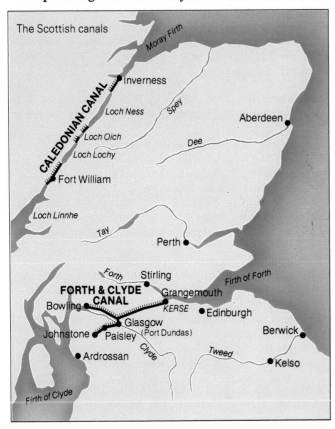

The Scottish canals

Moray Firth
CALEDONIAN CANAL
Inverness
Loch Ness
Spey
Aberdeen
Loch Oich
Dee
Loch Lochy
Fort William
Loch Linnhe
Tay
Perth
Forth
Stirling
Firth of Forth
FORTH & CLYDE CANAL
Bowling
Grangemouth
KERSE
Edinburgh
Glasgow
(Port Dundas)
Johnstone
Paisley
Berwick
Clyde
Tweed
Ardrossan
Kelso
Firth of Clyde

Worksection

Tradeways
Understand Your Work

The state of the roads and Turnpike Trusts
1 What were the roads like in dry weather?
2 What effect had this on carts?
3 How did rain affect the road surface?
4 How did the condition of the roads affect the cost of transport?
5 What were the only real means of transport in Scotland?
6 Why were the roads and bridges built by Wade not more helpful?
7 Did the Government try to help?
8 What now appeared along the roadways?
9 What was their purpose?

New Systems of Roadmaking
1 Whose method of roadmaking changed the appearance of the road gangs?
2 What change was there?
3 What was the main idea behind the new method?
4 Why did the water flow off the new roads to each side?
5 How was the road surface finally sealed?
6 Why did it not seep back underneath the surface?
7 Why was tar later added to the McAdam road?

Thomas Telford – Passengers and Mail
1 How did Telford's roads differ from those of McAdam?
2 What problems did he face in the Highlands?
3 What did Telford build in addition to roads?
4 Did he build these to the same design?
5 How did the work of McAdam and Telford affect transport?
6 How many coaches and horses were providing passenger and mail transport in Britain in the 1830s?
7 How long did the mail express take between London and Edinburgh?
8 How did the toll or inn-keeper know a coach was coming?
9 What increased the risk of accidents?
10 What risks did the passengers take on Britain's new turnpikes?
11 What effect did the heavy work of pulling coaches have on the horses?

The Navigators
1 Which goods were not carried on the new roads?
2 What new transport system was specially built for this purpose?
3 What was the first step in their construction?
4 When digging had begun, what were the surveyors checking?
5 How was the line and level kept in the face of rising ground, hollows or rocks?
6 How were the higher hills dealt with?
7 Why was clay applied to the sides and bottom of the trench?
8 How did James Watt's engines help in the work?
9 Where there had to be 'steps', how were these constructed?
10 What event was held to mark the opening day?
11 What kinds of place did the new network join together?
12 What made this a natural form of transport in Scotland?
13 What changes made it necessary to add the manmade waterways to the river system which had served the kingdom in the past?

The Forth and Clyde Canal
1 Who were the great engineers who built the canal system?
2 Were they canal builders only?
3 Where are examples of their work to be found?
4 Who directed the work on the Forth and Clyde Canal?
5 How many locks did it have?
6 How long did it take to complete?
7 How was the money for the canal found?
8 What was the town of Grangemouth originally called?
9 How did the canals help customers as well as business men?

Some Failures
1 What happened to the proposed canal joining Ardrossan to Glasgow?
2 How was it carried across the River Cart?
3 How was the high ground dealt with?
4 How many people died in the disaster?
5 Where and when did this happen?

The Caledonian Canal
1 Who was the engineer directing work on the Caledonian Canal?
2 Where does the canal begin and end?
3 How many miles of canal had to be dug to complete the waterway from the Atlantic Ocean to the North Sea?
4 What lochs does it join?
5 What special difficulties did Telford encounter while building the Caledonian Canal?
6 When was the canal opened?
7 How many men worked how long, to complete the canal?
8 What name is given to the set of locks which lead down from Loch Lochy towards Fort William?

Deepening the River and The Ports

1 Why were Glasgow merchants using down-river ports?
2 How far did the cargoes have to be carried to find water deep enough for ocean-going ships?
3 What name was given to this place?
4 How was the river deepened?
5 How did this affect the riverside in Glasgow?
6 What clues still remain to suggest that the Glasgow Clyde once flowed through soft and pleasant meadowland?
7 What work was now being carried out at the ports?
8 Where was Telford working?
9 What other engineers were involved?
10 How were the coasts being made safer?

Use Your Imagination

1 Why was it important, do you think, that Scotland developed a better system of transport?

2 Why do you suppose the condition of the roads was so bad?

3 What features of McAdam's system of road building were particularly attractive?

4 What is meant, do you suppose, by the statement – 'McAdam's roads are self-repairing'?

5 Do you think pebbles would be suitable for McAdam's roads?

6 What do you think is the most important thing in making a road?

7 What can you tell about the Highland countryside just from the figures given about miles of road compared with the number of bridges built by Telford?

8 Why do you suppose so many horses were needed for the coaches?

9 How do you think you might discover the distance between changes of horses on a coach journey?

10 Why was it so important to keep the canals level?

11 Why was it important to Glasgow that the Clyde should be deepened?

12 Do you think this is still true today?

13 What advantage would there be for ships in having the Caledonian Canal opened? Look at your map while you think about this.

14 What developments do you think may have made the Caledonian Canal less successful than was hoped?

Further Work

1 This is a set of rules laid down by Thomas Telford for the building of bridges. Read them carefully and discuss in your group why each of the rules was made and make notes of your group's ideas.

1 Keep to a straight line and have no bend in the road near the bridge.
2 Do not make bridges always the same width. On turnpike roads near large towns make bridges 40 feet wide; on country roads make bridges 30 to 36 feet wide. On small roads, bridges should be 20 to 24 feet wide.
3 The slope of the road over the bridge should be gentle. The gradient over a bridge should not be greater than 1 in 30.
4 Decide the number and width of the arches on the spot.
5 The arches must be wide enough to let all the water of the river, even in floodtime, flow underneath. Study other bridges on the river you are building over and ask the people about the floodwaters.
6 Dig into the ground and study the rocks under the river so that you build piers on firm rock.

2 Not all the dangers and discomforts of travel were caused by the road surface or the jolting coach – particularly at night. Think about this and try to imagine what sort of thing might happen as you make your way through the darkening forest. Write a little story about your experience. Start like this –
'Progress was easy on the good sand road, but the thickening trees closed out the moonlight and it grew very dark' . . .

3 One particular danger of the roads was the highwayman, the cloaked, masked figure looming up like a ghost in the moonlight to demand at pistol point, 'Your money or your life!' Your class could make a large picture of such a person, like this –

a Each person completely covers an A4 sheet of paper in his/her idea of a 'night' colour. These are put together to form a large patchwork of the night. Pin this background to the wall at working height.
b On another piece of paper each person draws their own highwayman. From the best of these the 'design' of the highwayman for the big picture is decided and enlarged using a grid to match the grid of the night rectangles.
c Very lightly in white chalk, sketch outline only of the full size highwayman on the background (No features or details – just silhouette outline).
d Thin strips of white paper (1 cm wide) are then cut to stick over the chalk line and give the finished ghostly effect of the night rider as a white outline against the dark sky.
e Add a moon in white paper if you think this improves the finished ghostlike effect.

You will enjoy reading the poems called '*The Highwayman*' and '*Dick Turpin's Ride*' by Alfred Noyes after completing your picture.

The Victorians

During the Victorian years Scotland grew very rapidly. The eighteen year old queen came to the throne on the death of her uncle, William IV, in 1837, and by then two and a half million people lived in the northern kingdom. Most of them were townsfolk. The better farming methods produced more food but used less labour. It was in the factories and mills, the ironworks and coalfields that work was to be found and wages earned. The industrial towns grew larger and the country villages fewer and quieter. Now the four cities of Glasgow, Edinburgh, Dundee and Aberdeen housed more than half a million people and they were still expanding. The figure would double inside a generation.

There were better roads now in Scotland, and the canals too – a proper transport system to serve the growing nation. There was plenty of coal for energy and James Watt's engines to turn its heat to steam-power, and drive its machines. And there was iron to build with, two hundred and fifty thousand tons of it each year, streaming from seventy blast furnaces, to be cast and forged by the ironmasters. Everything needed for a great engineering industry was to hand in central Scotland, and Lanarkshire in particular.

Engineering

This wealth of material and power had been in supply for some years. But there was still one item missing, something without which the whole idea of modern engineering is unthinkable. For centuries men had crafted exquisitely and delicately in brass and wood. The material had been fashioned for spindles and wheels much as the potter shapes the clay spinning on his wheel. For brass or wood the 'potter's wheel' was placed on its side and called a lathe. For the potter's fingers the turner used the cutting edge of a chisel. Both men depended on their steadiness of hand and judgment of eye. But now it was iron that turned on the lathe, a material whose very strength made for hard and slow work.

And the type and scale of the work had completely changed. Long iron rods, machined straight and true, were required for the great beam engines. The turners had now to hold the cutting tool steady as they moved from one end of the rod to the other. Only the high craftsmen, and there were never enough of them, might attempt such tasks and even then they had only limited success. James Watt had to be content with a fit between rod and cylinder top, between cylinder wall and piston side, through which a coin could easily pass. The gap was made good with a packing of hemp. And for this crude arrangement he had waited five years. Not until John Wilkinson devised a machine in 1774 that could bore out the cylinder even to this rough standard, did Watt's engine work at all!

But already the problem was being tackled. In London a blacksmith called Maudsley had taken the cutting edge out of the turner's hand and clamped it firmly in the jaws of a toolpost. The toolpost he set on the perfectly straight and true surfaces of a slideway where it would travel the whole length of the lathe, and towards the whirling iron or away from it. As the cutting tool made its perfect passes shaving off layer after layer a dead true rod was produced exact in size and identical with any other turned to match it. At last a perfect fit was assured.

Maudsley's lathe

Henry Maudsley did more. He constructed machines to bore and slot, to plane and shape. He made special tools to machine special parts; a whole set, for example, to make the blocks for ships' hoisting tackle. They would now be turned out at a hundred and sixty thousand per year, using only ten men instead of a hundred and ten as before. All this was measured, not to the thickness of a coin, but to one fortieth part of a millimetre, a thousandth of an inch. Maudsley had brought the missing part to the industry of mechanical engineering – accuracy. And through his machines, he put it in the hands of the factory floor worker and not just the high craftsman. Now precision engineering would be for all. The great philosopher-economist, Adam Smith's example of mass produced pins in his *Wealth of Nations* would be followed for a huge range of products. His warning about the dullness of mind and spirit that must come to those condemned to spend their lives 'in performing a few simple operations' without 'occasion to exert their understanding' was forgotten in such a dazzling prospect of more and more profit.

Broomielaw, Clydeside, in the mid-19th century

A Revolution in Transport

With such machinery the Victorians were ready to expand industrial Scotland and once more it was transport that held the key. The existing network of roads and canals worked well enough, but still very slowly. Now would come a system to sweep aside the canals and, for half a century, the roads too.

In a yard in Port Glasgow a new vessel was built. It was different from anything that had been seen before. And she caused a sensation when, in 1812, she butted her way upriver to Glasgow. Not only did the *Comet* look different with her strangely thick 'mast' from which hung the yard arm of a square sail, but from the mast was pouring black smoke as she thrashed the foaming water with the pairs of revolving paddles under her bulging skirts at each side. To many she was a creation of the devil, but Henry Bell's *Comet*, built by John Wood & Son, was simply the first passenger carrying steamship. Within a decade there would be a hundred more built on the Clyde and Forth to trade along the coast and with Ireland. Steam power had arrived in transport.

And not just on the sea. On the land too there were equally surprising sights. Carriages that moved without horses, steam carriages shared the turnpikes with the stage coaches. They were not popular, and grew even less so when one exploded at Paisley killing five passengers, the very first fatal 'automobile' accident. Yet steam would find its place in land transport.

The First 'Railways'

For a very long time people had known that the quickest and cheapest way to make a very good road on which to pull trucks was to lay two very smooth, very narrow strips of roadway just the right distance apart to match the wheels. They made these waggonways of stone or wood, and by the end of the eighteenth century, of iron. Along the waggonways trains of loaded trucks were drawn by teams of horses far more easily than on ordinary roads because there was so little friction between iron wheel and iron rail.

A horse-drawn railway truck

'Locomotion'

In the same year as the *Comet* was making her maiden voyage on the Clyde another 'steamer' was being prepared for trials in England at Newcastle-upon-Tyne. But it was neither on riverway nor highway. William Medley's *Puffing Billy* pulled its wagons on rails. Some years later on the 27th September 1825, George Stephenson's tiny engine, *Locomotion*, pulled out from Darlington with more than a hundred metres of waggons behind it, carrying five hundred passengers, and puffed steadily to Stockton twenty seven miles away where it was saluted by booming cannon and brass bands, waving flags and cheering crowds. The age of the steam railway had begun.

The opening of the Stockton to Darlington line in 1825

The 'Navvies'

In Scotland there were already several railways running between coalfields, ironworks, and town. They were horse-drawn and served mainly the coal industry. The route from the Monklands pits to Kirkintilloch cut by half the cost of Glasgow's coal and was converted to steam in 1832. But it was the Victorians who really put the country on the rails. And again all over the country it was much the same as in the canal digging days. There were the engineers to plan and survey the routes; to design and direct the making of bridges and embankments, cuttings and tunnels, and the laying of the track. The workforce itself was the same as before – the 'navvies', short for 'navigators',

who had laboured on the great canal projects. They prepared the road for the rails with pick and shovel, each moving eight to ten tons of earth in a shift. Though this roadway did not have to be dead level like the canal bed only gentle slopes and gentle curves could be allowed. When it was ready a deep layer of gravel was spread in which to bed the heavy wooden sleepers. On each sleeper two cast iron 'chairs' were fitted to hold the rails gripped tight by wooden wedges hammered home between rail and chair. And because the heat of the sun and the chill of frost would expand and contract the iron rails, small gaps were left between each rail and the next to prevent buckling. The rails were then joined by fish-plates bolted on to each side through oblong holes which allowed slide as the iron lengthened or shortened in the changing temperature.

By 1838, passenger and goods lines ran between: Glasgow and Edinburgh; Paisley and Greenock; Glasgow, Paisley, Kilmarnock and Ayr. Day trips to the capital and sea-side holidays were now possible for the Victorian Scots.

And still the railways grew. All Britain was victim to railway mania. Everywhere lines were being laid by different companies to different widths. Scotland's Solicitor General, Henry Cockburn, said that it was 'an island of lunatics, all railway mad. The patients are raving even in the wild recesses of the Highlands.' But out of this Victorian madness came Britain's great railway system.

By 1850 there were more than six thousand miles of track carrying trains to all the major towns and cities: from Glasgow to London, London to Aberdeen; fast and on time. The main turnpikes could not compete and the clatter of the stage coach and the hooting post horn fell silent. The bustling wayside inns grew quiet and the toll keepers with their gates were seldom disturbed. But some roads could work with the new faster transport service. They carried the traffic to and from the railway station just as the roads served the canal system. Local roads and carters thrived, trunk roads and long distance carriers went down. In time the canals too gave way.

And still the railways grew. Twenty thousand miles of track reached into every corner of Britain by the end of the Victorian Age in 1901. Trains raced along their shining rails not at the mail coach average speed of 9 m.p.h., but 90 m.p.h. A thousand million passengers were carried in a year on the railways of Britain and five hundred million tons of goods, coal, and ore.

Caledonian Railway Locomotive No. 123, built 1886

Shipping

Shipping was growing too. Steamships were in regular service across the seas and oceans and in local waters, on the Clyde and Forth, and around the coast. Great shipping lines like Cunard and P & O were now in business and ordering new ships from the Clydeside yards at Govan, Whiteinch and Dumbarton, at Renfrew, Port Glasgow and Greenock. Just as sail had given way to steam, wood gave way to iron, and iron in its time, to steel. Glasgow flourished and the Clyde prospered. They were Britain's leading centres of shipbuilding and heavy engineering. They overtook London and served the new transport systems of land and sea, here and abroad. Great new firms grew out of smaller ones – Fairfield's Shipbuilding and Engineering Company, Beardmores and the famous John Brown's, later to build the greatest ocean liners in the world, the *Queen Mary*, *Queen Elizabeth*, and *QE2* and many others.

A Clydeside launch; the QE2

At the close of the Victorian Age more than four hundred thousand Scots worked in the shipyards and engineering factories, in the coalfields and iron and steel works. This was now twice as many as worked on the land. In 1812 the Clyde produced the little *Comet* and ninety years later was constructing half a million tons of shipping a year. The nation's wealth came now, not from its farms or textile mills, but from the heavy industries. And it prospered.

The State of the Cities

At least some of the nation prospered. Again Adam Smith's advice that 'those who created the nation's wealth by their own labour should have a proper share of it,' went unheeded. Robert Owen's shining example was not followed. For all Scotland's new found riches the greater part of her people suffered grinding miserable poverty. All lived under the shadow of epidemic cholera, typhus, small-pox and tuberculosis, which spread easily and wildly from the ugly squalor of the teeming slums to the pleasant richer quarters.

Scotland's towns had grown up too fast for their councils to cope with the expansion. In the first half of the nineteenth century, Aberdeen's population shot up from twenty-seven thousand to seventy-two thousand; Edinburgh, from eighty-three thousand to almost two hundred thousand; Dundee, from twenty-six thousand to eighty thousand; and Glasgow, from seventy-seven thousand to a huge three hundred and forty-five thousand. By the end of the century one Scot in six would live in the great Clydeside city. Housing, water supply, and sanitation fell hopelessly behind and, more than ever, the towns were breeding grounds for disease. A third of the people in this prosperous kingdom of the north lived in one-roomed dwellings and a fair number of these tiny flats and houses had no windows. About fifteen hundred of Edinburgh's 'single ends' had no fewer than six and as many as fifteen people crowded into their dismal shelter – including lodgers. The miserable dwellings were huddled in towering heaps, as many as sixty opening off one steep dark stairway: two hundred and fifty folk crammed into the dirt and decay of the tall tenements without water supply or sanitation.

And Glasgow grew worse. The once 'beautifullest little city in Britain' was now called instead 'possibly the filthiest and unhealthiest of all British towns' by Edwin Chadwick in a report on the condition of workers. In another report another inspector said, 'I have seen human degredation in some of its worst phases but I can advisedly say that I did not believe, until I visited the wynds of Glasgow that so large an amount of filth, crime, misery and disease existed on one spot in any civilised country.' The great new wealth of Scotland was certainly not being shared by those whose labour had created it.

A Glasgow Court in the 19th century

Improvements

But already things were beginning to change. In 1832 the number of people allowed to vote in the General Election was increased. The following year the composition of the town councils were altered. Now, each year, one third of the council were required to resign, and stand for re-election if they wished. Councillors would need to please the electors, and keep their promises, if they hoped to be voted in again. The quality of people serving on councils soon improved. And by the end of the century all men would have the vote, and Scotland would send not fifty-three M.P.'s to Westminster, but seventy-two. She would have a bigger say in the affairs of Great Britain.

A Trade Union meeting and (**right**) the Emblem of the Scottish Typographical Association c1882

Trade Unions

The workers themselves were fighting back against the awful conditions under which they lived and toiled. In the mines and mills, in the shipyards and in the factories men of the same trade were banding together to stand up from their rights, and to begin the long struggle for their proper share of the wealth their labour created. Trade Unions of spinners and weavers, of miners and metal workers, builders and railwaymen were determined to improve the wretched conditions and wages of the working man. To begin with they were weak and badly organised. Their strikes were uncertain and usually collapsed, the men defeated and forced to return to the same or worse wages. The employers had wealth. The law and the courts were on their side and there was a great pool of cheap Irish labour with which to break the strikes if necessary. The Unions had nothing. But in time their strength grew and with it a hatred for those who had fixed them in stark poverty. Had Robert Owen's gentler, wiser advice been taken, much of the bitterness that followed and still lingers today, could have been avoided and the nation would have benefited.

The Water Companies

The new better councils now had to face the huge problems of overcrowded towns and cities. Perhaps because it was so bad, Glasgow acted first and most boldly. In the face of angry and determined opposition from the private water companies who had failed for years to meet Glasgow's need, the City Corporation asked for Parliament's consent to a grand new scheme. To help win approval, the councillors employed Robert Stephenson, (son of the *Rocket*'s inventor), and the great Isambard Kingdom Brunel as advisers. And win they did. In 1855 the mighty work began – thirty-five miles from Glasgow. After four years of solid labour the task was done. On the 14th October 1859, Queen Victoria turned the valve that brought Loch Katrine's clear water to the heart of the city, thirty-seven million gallons of it a day. It was Britain's finest water supply.

When the deadly cholera and typhus plagues swept through Britain in 1832, four thousand died in Glasgow. In 1849 and again in 1854, the same number perished. But in 1866, after Loch Katrine's water had begun to flow from the city's taps, when the plague came again and thousands died in Greenock, not twenty miles away, of Glasgow's half million people, only fifty-five lost their lives.

A map of Glasgow's water supply system

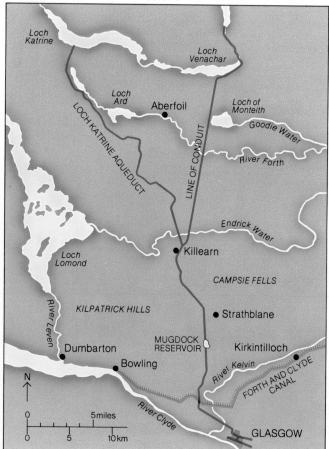

Houses

Now the Corporation turned to housing. In the same year that the new water supply saved Glasgow from disease, the City Improvement Trust was formed and began at once to clear the slums. Old decaying houses were demolished and new wide streets laid. But times were hard and those builders who tried found they could not make a profit. The Trust took back the unwanted land and by 1901 had covered it in new houses, fifteen hundred good quality flats in four storey tenements. And that same year the Lord Provost declared that 'the cry of the unhoused and the insufficiently housed is one which neither as individual citizens nor as a municipality, and neither as humanitarians nor as Christians can we afford to neglect.' There was, of course, the usual batch of well-to-do merchants and industrialists who thought the corporation could and should afford to neglect the cry. Against their bitter opposition and with the Lord Provost's noble words still ringing in the City Chambers, Glasgow bent to the task of housing its people just as Robert Owen had proposed seventy years before, in Scotland's first council houses.

Fiat lux

In 1792 a Scotsman called William Murdoch, who worked with James Watt, took some coal dust and sprinkled it into the bowl of his clay pipe. He then placed the pipe on the fire – and lit up the world, though he started with his own house in Redruth, Cornwall. He had invented gaslight and Glasgow was eager to have it. The Private Gas Light Company was formed in 1818, but their prices were too high for ordinary folk. Only when the Corporation took over in 1869 was the cost lowered.

Out and About

In the same year the Corporation began road works of a new kind. Everywhere along the centre of Glasgow's main streets rails were being laid between the cobbles. Along these Corporation tracks would run a new vehicle – the horse-drawn tramway car. At first the service was operated by a private company but in 1894 the Corporation took over. Improvements were made at once, lower fares for the public and shorter hours for the drivers and conductors, better conditions for the horses and cleaner vehicles. Six years later the system became electric and Glasgow had its famous trams, swaying and lurching through the city with bells clanging and iron wheels grinding on the rails. By night their windows brightened the streets and the flashes of dazzling blue from their overhead cables lit up the sky. The Glasgow trams were Europe's best and the city's favourite transport service.

There were the Corporation Parks too, where people found room to breathe and run free in their crowded city, and to play their national games. It was in Queen's Park that one of Scotland's first major football clubs was formed in 1867, taking the park's name for it's own. Queen's Park F.C. did a great deal to lay down firm rules for the game, refusing to play teams who were unwilling to abide by them. Rangers and Celtic, Heart of Midlothian and Hibernian followed quickly and brought bitter religious feelings into the sport, feelings more to do with cheap Irish labour and out-of-work or striking Scots. Shamefully, they linger on.

It was a mighty city, Victorian Glasgow, already one sixth part of Scotland and world famed for its engineering and enterprise. When the Grand Duke Alexis of Russia came to the launching of the Czar's royal yacht he exclaimed in admiration at all he saw, insisting that Glasgow was the 'centre of intelligence of England'. No one present thought to disagree.

Gas lighting and trams in turn of the century Glasgow

An Age of Progress

Where Glasgow led, the rest of Scotland would follow though not always with the same energy. Water supplies and sanitation, street lighting and transport, housing and recreation were all improved as the century wore on. And education too was better provided for. Now, just as John Knox had dreamed three centuries before, schooling would be for all children in every parish and burgh, compulsory and free. It was in the Scottish tradition to educate alike rich and poor, high and low. Now it was law. There had never been in Scotland that straw-haired, straw-chewing country yokel of England, ignorant for the want of a chance to be educated. Instead there was the 'lad o' pairts' who, though poor, was talented and attended schools that were truly public with the aid of monies set aside for that purpose. The crofter's son and the laird's sat side by side to the benefit of both and of the whole nation. Now the law would ensure that this could continue, though less worthy ambitions and traditions would yet separate the high born from the low.

It had been a great age of progress, the long reign of Queen Victoria, and when it ended in 1901, the workshops of the northern kingdom were serving the world. Scotland prospered. The lifestyle of the people had more in common with ours today than with that of the early years of the nineteenth century. The nation was modern and confident, looking eagerly towards the bright promise of the new century.

Worksection

The Victorians
Understand Your Work

Engineering
1 How much iron was being produced in Scotland around 1837?
2 Which Queen came to the throne in that year?
3 Which was the best area of Scotland for the development of the engineering industry?
4 What machine was used for making spindles and wheels?
5 Why was iron more difficult to shape than brass?
6 How did Henry Maudsley solve the problem of making straight rods of iron on the lathe?
7 What missing item did Maudsley bring to engineering?
8 How accurate were his machines?
9 How did this alter the type of person required to produce high quality parts?
10 What part of modern industry had Maudsley made possible?
11 What was forgotten in the 'dazzling prospect of more and more profit'?

A Revolution in Transport
1 What was wrong with Scotland's transport system at this time?
2 What was unusual.about the 'Comet'?
3 What pushed the 'Comet' through the water?
4 Was the 'Comet' popular with everybody?
5 What now appeared on the roads of Scotland for the first time?
6 What happened to make the new arrivals even more unpopular?
7 When was 'Puffing Billy's' trial run?
8 What happened on the 27th September, 1825?
9 Of what was this the beginning?

The 'Navvies'
1 Were railways new to the Scottish coalfields?
2 Where did the navvies get their name?
3 What was the first stage in laying the rails for the new steam trains?
4 What were the rails fixed to?
5 Why were gaps left between the end of each length of rail and the next?
6 How were the rail ends kept together yet able to move slightly?
7 What effect did the new railways have on other forms of transport?
8 Why did some parts of the road transport system thrive?
9 How many passengers were being carried on the railway system by the end of the Victorian Age?

The State of the Cities
1 What effect was the new steam power industry having on the Clydeside?
2 What famous ships were built at John Brown's?
3 How did this change the employment of the people?
4 Whose advice and example were being ignored?
5 What quality of life did the ordinary people have during this time of great prosperity?
6 What proportion of the nation lived in Glasgow?
7 What proportion of Scots lived in single roomed houses?
8 How was Glasgow now described?
9 What was certainly not happening to Victorian Scotland's wealth?
10 What change in the election procedure made town councillors wish to please the people?
11 How did Scotland's representation at Westminster change during this century?

Trade Unions and the Water Companies
1 How did Trade Unions come into being?
2 What problems did they face in the early years?
3 What advantages did the employers have over the unions?
4 What was Glasgow's first major improvement scheme?
5 Who opposed the new plans?
6 Which engineers advised Glasgow in its great project?
7 What effect did the Loch Katrine water have when the plagues of typhus and cholera swept Britain in 1866?
8 How did this compare with Greenock?
9 What did the Corporation tackle next?
10 Who opposed the scheme to build Scotland's first council houses?
11 Why did the Corporation have to take over the gas lighting of Glasgow?

Out and About
1 When were the trams electrified?
2 When did the Corporation take over the running of the trams?
3 Was it a popular service?
4 Why were parks provided?
5 What special contribution did Queen's Park F.C. make to the game of football?
6 What bad effect did football teams with a religious following have on the life of the cities?

An Age of Progress
1 What Victorian developments helped the nation to be healthier?
2 How was education improved?
3 How did the traditions of Scottish education differ from the English ones?
4 What good features of the system was later to be lost?
5 In what areas of work was Scotland making a worldwide contribution?

Use Your Imagination

1 Why do you think the early engines were bound to be very inefficient?

2 In what ways do you suppose the moving tool post was better than the human hand?

3 Henry Maudsley's inventions took much of the craft out of metal work. Do you think craftsmen were no longer needed as a result?

4 What part of modern industrial practice did the work of Maudsley make possible, do you think?

5 How did this alter the life of the people?

6 Why do you think the steam driven automobile was never a real success and yet this system worked well for road rollers?

7 What do you suppose attracted passengers to steam travel?

8 How did the nation increase its wealth by manufacturing and mining? Where did the money come from?

9 Who do you think really caused the rise of the Trade Union movement?

10 What effect do you think it has had on the lives of the people of this country?

11 What do you suspect was the cause of great epidemics of typhus and cholera?

12 What developments in the nineteenth century show that at least some people were caring about the condition of the common people?

Further Work

1 A piston and cylinder is one way to turn steampower into mechanical energy and it is fine for pumps, but not so good for wheels. How else do you think you could use steam to turn things without all the rods and shafts? Discuss this in your group and make a drawing of your invention. Thinking how windpower is used might help you in your design. (No experiments please – steam is far too dangerous!)

2 The railways took the traffic away from the roads and the toll gates fell into disuse. Here is a poem by John Drinkwater called '*The Toll-Gate House*' for you to enjoy which describes how things have changed and how the old toll keeper now lives:

> The toll-gate's gone, but still stands lone,
> In the dip of the hill, the house of stone,
> And over the roof in the branching pine
> The great owl sits in the white moonshine.
> An old man lives, and lonely, there,
> His windows yet on the cross-roads stare,
> And on Michaelmas night in all the years
> A galloping far and faint he hears . . .
> His casement open wide he flings
> With 'Who goes there?' and a lantern swings . . .
> But never more in the dim moonbeam
> Than a cloak and a plume and the silver gleam
> Of passing spurs in the night can he see,
> For the toll-gate's gone, and the road is free.

3 From the figures given for the growth of Scotland's city populations you can prepare a graph. Show the dates on the horizontal axis and the population on the vertical axis. Make a rough graph first so that you can find out what units suit the size of your paper. The final version can be displayed for others to see. You could make other graphs to show the development of other features of the nation so that they can be compared.

4 '*Night Mail*' by W.H. Auden describes the overnight-train north. Try to find a copy of this splendid poem and practise saying it aloud in your group. It could be done section by section, each member reading a portion and when you are satisfied with your efforts you might make a tape recording.

The first Victorian